HOW TO BE A BETTER STUDENT

J. Wayne Wrightstone

Former Assistant Superintendent for Research
Board of Education of the City of New York

SCIENCE RESEARCH ASSOCIATES, INC.
Chicago, Palo Alto, Toronto, Henley-on-Thames, Sydney
A Subsidiary of IBM

ACKNOWLEDGMENTS

The author and the publisher wish to express their gratitude for the courtesy and cooperation shown by the following publishers who were kind enough to grant permission for the use of the selections in this book:

Chapter 7
The Sandburg quotation is from "Fog" in *Chicago Poems* by Carl Sandburg, published by Harcourt Brace Jovanovich, Inc.
The Brooke quotation is from "The Great Lover" in *The Collected Poems of Rupert Brooke,* © 1915 by Dodd, Mead & Co. By permission of the publisher, McClelland and Stewart Ltd., and Sidgwick and Jackson Ltd.

Chapter 8
The road map is a section of a New England highway map, © 1971 by General Drafting Co., Inc.
The bar graph on languages of the world and the chart on work-time are from the *World Almanac 1971.*
The photograph is from American Telephone and Telegraph Co.
Drawing by Frascino, © 1968 The New Yorker Magazine, Inc.

Chapter 9
The dictionary entry is from *Webster's Seventh New Collegiate Dictionary,* © 1971 by G. & C. Merriam Co., publishers of the Merriam-Webster Dictionaries.

Chapter 10
The library classification is reproduced from Abridged Edition 10, 1971 of *DEWEY Decimal Classification* by permission of Forest Press, Inc., owner of copyright.

CONTENTS

1 • Why Become a Better Student?   5

2 • What Is the Best Way to Learn?   11

3 • How Can You Improve
Your Memory and Understanding?   17

4 • On Your Mark, Get Set — Study!   23

5 • How Well Do You Read?   27

6 • How Well Do You Listen?   35

7 • Write It Right!   39

8 • How Do You Read — without Words?   49

9 • Look It Up!   59

10 • Off to the Library!   65

11 • Taking Notes, Making Outlines   73

12 • Think It Through!   77

13 • How Can You Best Participate in Classwork?   85

14 • How Can You Best Prepare for and Take Tests?   91

1•why become a better student?

Can you become a better student? The answer is *yes*. Whether you are a poor student, an average student, or a good student, *you can become a better student*. And as a better student you will get much more out of your studies — and enjoy them more, too.

As a better student, will you have to spend more time studying, or study harder than you do now?

Probably not. A good student usually spends fewer hours and puts in less effort studying than the poorer student does.

What is the most important difference between a good student and a poor one? Simply that the good student has and uses effective study skills, habits, and attitudes. He plans his study or an assignment and then follows through until he finishes it. He concentrates on what he is studying; he doesn't allow anyone or anything to interrupt. The poor student, on the other hand, shifts from one study activity to another. He lets his mind wander. He is easily distracted by anyone who comes along.

Some people are born with greater ability to learn than others, but poor study habits can make a poor student out of the brightest person. Good study habits will help any student — poor, average, or good — make the most of his abilities.

This book will help you develop the study habits and attitudes a good student must have. It will help you learn to study more effectively and more successfully.

How Can You Become a Better Student?

You may ask, "Can I learn to study better by reading a book?" In one experiment students who took a how-to-study course gained 45 percent in their average grades in English, social studies, mathematics, science, and other subjects. Students with similar abilities who did not take the study course gained only 7 percent.

No matter how good a student you are *now*, you can improve. You can, for example, learn to do the following things:

1. *Concentrate* on what you're studying. Refuse to daydream.

2. Make a *study schedule* and keep it. Don't skip from one study activity to another.

3. *Skim* the whole assignment and then study it for details. Don't start by reading the whole assignment slowly and laboriously, without an idea of the overall meaning.

4. Acquire the important *study skills* in a planned order instead of learning them in a hit-or-miss way.

In each chapter of this book you'll learn about the study skills that can help you become a more successful student. You should read each chapter thoroughly and do each practice exercise carefully.

Why Become a Better Student?

It's a good question. Being a good student takes time and effort. Why bother?

One good reason is that being a poor student usually takes at least as much work as being a good one. A poor student who hasn't studied his assignments regularly is faced with a huge cramming job the night before an exam. He may stay up most of the night making a tremendous effort to master the material at the last moment. He probably won't succeed. The good student, on the other hand, spreads the same amount of effort over a period of days, with only a quick review at the end. He doesn't have to exhaust himself by cramming, and so he will probably do better in the exam than the poor student who crammed. He didn't do much more work, either.

Here are some other reasons for becoming a better student:

1. If you learn to study more effectively, you will learn more and increase your understanding of the world you live in. This, in turn, will contribute to your growth as an individual.

2. If you learn to study better and improve your schoolwork on your own, you'll feel more and more able to stand on your own feet. You'll become more independent.

3. If you learn to study better, you'll have more free time for other activities—sports, reading, dates, community projects.

4. Finally, if you learn to study more effectively, you'll have a better chance to succeed in later work, whether in school or college or in a career. You'll develop study skills, habits, and attitudes that will serve you well all through your life. If you are successful in your courses, you'll build confidence in your abilities, and this confidence will help you succeed in other things.

Study Is Self-Directed Learning

The difference between a good student and a poor one is mostly a difference in capacity to study efficiently and effectively. In short, the better you direct or manage your learning, the better student you will be.

How Can You Manage Your Study Activities?

This book offers many suggestions on how to study, but only *you* can learn to manage your study activities. If you have poor study habits, you should replace them with good ones, including the habit of concentration. You should develop skills on the subjects in which you are weak, through practice.

As your own study manager, you may have to work hard at first to study better. After a while,

though, you'll find that studying is becoming easier and that the results are worth the time and effort you've put in.

What Are Study Activities?

If you ask most students, "What are study activities?" they'll probably answer, "Reading assignments and doing homework."

If you think about it, though, you'll realize that studying includes not only reading and doing homework, but *any* activity through which you obtain or give information and ideas. While you're studying you may be *reading* a book. You may be *listening* to a teacher or to another student. You may be *writing* a report or *speaking* to the class.

While you're studying you may be looking for information or judging the soundness of information you already have. You may be organizing ideas—your own and other people's. All these are study activities that you carry on from day to day in your schoolwork.

Some nonstudent activities can also contribute to what you are learning. For example, when you study American history, you may recall a movie you've seen about the life of Abraham Lincoln—a movie that helped you understand certain events. You may see a TV program about weather, a subject you are studying in general science. You may meet an interesting person. You may travel to a national park or to some other place of natural beauty. You may listen to a record. Then you can draw on any of these experiences for an essay topic in English class.

You may read a newspaper and realize how the events of the present are shaped by events of the past that you studied in history class. You may learn about practical citizenship by taking part in a voter-registration drive.

If you think actively about what you're seeing, hearing, and doing, you are adding to your background of experience. You are sharpening your ability to read and listen to the ideas of others and to speak and write intelligently about them. In short, you are studying!

You can fill your storehouse of knowledge through study and study-related activities. You can draw on this storehouse for facts and ideas at any time. Through study activities you can also develop your reading and other skills. With greater knowledge and improved skills you'll do better work in your courses.

Spend time each week building up your general background of knowledge, as well as developing specific knowledge of your school subjects. That is, try to balance the two kinds of knowledge-getting activities.

A Checklist of Study Abilities

The checklist that follows gives you a preview of the topics this book will discuss. It will also help you rate your study abilities—your skills, habits, and attitudes.

You will fill in this checklist twice—now, at the beginning of the book, and later, when you have completed the exercises in the book. When you compare the two sets of checks, you'll have a way to determine your progress in developing the study skills you need.

What study abilities do you have? Which do you lack? To find out, read each statement carefully. Then, to the right of each statement, make a check in the column that describes your interests, habits, and skills, as follows:

- Almost never (0 to 9 percent of the time)
- Seldom (10 to 29 percent of the time)
- Sometimes (30 to 69 percent of the time)
- Usually (70 to 89 percent of the time)
- Nearly always (90 to 100 percent of the time)

A CHECKLIST OF YOUR STUDY ABILITIES

HOW DO YOU RATE YOURSELF ON STUDY ABILITY?

Now, as you are beginning this book, mark your checks in these columns.

Later, when you have finished this book, mark your checks in these columns.

A. Statements of abilities	Almost never	Seldom	Sometimes	Usually	Nearly always	Almost never	Seldom	Sometimes	Usually	Nearly always
1. I am interested in my school courses.										
2. I have tried to master the basic ideas and skills in each of my courses.										
3. From time to time, I practice or review what I have learned in a course.										
4. I get satisfaction from learning.										
5. When I study, I clear extra things off the desk or table.										
6. When I study, I avoid such distractions as talking, radio, and television.										
7. I write down the assignments to be studied.										
8. I make and keep a time schedule for study.										
9. I scan the whole assignment. Then I study the parts in detail.										

	Almost never	Seldom	Sometimes	Usually	Nearly always		Almost never	Seldom	Sometimes	Usually	Nearly always
10. As I listen to an oral presentation, I get the main ideas.											
11. As I hear a lecture, I recognize the important details.											
12. As I listen to a lecture, I follow the organization of the speaker's ideas.											
13. As I listen to a lecture, I draw my own conclusion from what the speaker has said.											
14. Before I write on a topic, I take notes on cards or notebook paper.											
15. After taking notes I organize them into an outline.											
16. I write my first draft of a theme or report on a topic rapidly and then revise this draft.											
17. I read reference books at about 250 to 300 words a minute.											
18. I try to increase my vocabulary of English words.											
19. In reading I can find the main idea of a paragraph.											
20. In reading I can find the supporting ideas of a paragraph.											
21. I know how to read and understand maps, graphs, and tables.											
22. I can interpret cartoons and pictures.											
23. I know how to use contents, index, appendix, glossary, other informational aids in a book.											
24. I know how to use such library aids as the Dewey decimal system.											

	Now, mark your checks here:					Later, mark your checks here:				
	Almost never	Seldom	Sometimes	Usually	Nearly always	Almost never	Seldom	Sometimes	Usually	Nearly always
25. I know how to use the library card-catalog files.										
26. I know how to use encyclopedias and other reference books.										
27. I know how to use the *Readers' Guide to Periodical Literature.*										
28. I am familiar with the dictionary and use it when I need it.										
29. In my study assignments I use newspapers, magazines, radio, and TV.										
30. I take notes on large loose-leaf notebook paper.										
31. In taking rough notes I abbreviate words.										
32. For each of my courses I use a different section of my notebook.										
33. For each course I review my notes daily and make a summary.										
34. Before writing a report or composition I make an outline of it.										
35. I organize my outline so that both main ideas and subordinate ideas are clear.										
36. I look for prejudice in sources of information.										
37. I look for "tricks" in reasoning used by some writers and speakers.										
38. I know how to add up facts and draw sound conclusions.										
39. I work well with a committee, either as an ordinary member or as the chairman.										

Almost never	Seldom	Sometimes	Usually	Nearly always		Almost never	Seldom	Sometimes	Usually	Nearly always
0	1	2	3	4		0	1	2	3	4

40. I participate actively in class recitations and discussions.

41. I behave courteously in the classroom.

42. I prepare for examinations by doing my work day by day.

43. I prepare for an examination by reviewing my notebook and textbook.

44. In answering examination questions I plan my time.

45. I answer essay questions in a systematic way. I organize my ideas. I write legibly and correctly.

46. I know how to follow the instructions for taking objective tests — for instance, multiple-choice, matching, true-false, and fill-in-the-blank items.

B. **Total number of checks in a column**

_____

C. **Number of points for each check in a column**

_____

D. **Study-ability score — number of checks (B) times number of points (C)**

_____

E. **Total score (total number of points in five columns)**

Now _____   Later _____

After you figure out your total score in the five columns headed "Now," reread each of the statements that you checked "Almost never" or "Seldom." These are the study abilities in which you need most to improve yourself.

More Things to Do to Improve Your Study Skills

1. Think about your reasons for wishing to become a better student.

2. List the ways in which you think you might improve.

3. Write a short statement about how you manage your study activities. Include both strong and weak points.

4. List your out-of-school activities that can contribute to the various school subjects you are studying.

2•WHAT IS THE BEST WAY TO LEARN?

Learning is one of the most important things anyone does. Because people can learn, they have explored vast continents, written symphonies, invented lifesaving medicines, and traveled to the moon and toward the stars.

Most people learn more things in more places than they realize—at home, at school, at the factory or office. They keep on learning all through life.

Because learning is so fundamental to living, psychologists have studied how we learn. Their experiments have uncovered the techniques by which a person can learn most effectively. Helping you understand and apply these techniques toward becoming a better student is the main purpose of this chapter.

Exactly Why Do You Want to Learn?

Do you have strong motives—reasons—for learning? You might have some of these motives: to satisfy curiosity; to increase personal growth; to win praise from parents, teachers, or friends; to build a basis for success in college or in a job. If you have strong motives for learning, you'll be more interested in your school courses. You'll also make a greater effort to learn as much as possible.

Naturally, you learn best when you have a definite goal in mind. For example, if mountain climbing is your goal, you'll be eager to learn the basic skills of that sport. You'll learn well—and fast. If you're not really interested in mountain climbing, though, you'll practice the needed skills in a dull and mechanical way. You'll learn them slowly, if ever.

If your career goal is to become an engineer, you have a powerful motive to learn mathematics and science. If you hope to become an English or a history teacher, you have a strong motive to do well in those two subjects.

A person learns best the things in which he is interested.

Which Subjects Interest You Most?

To indicate your interest in each of your school subjects, rank them according to how much you like them. Write a 1 at the left of the subject you like best, a 2 at the left of the subject you like second best, and so on through 11.

_____English	_____Art	_____Music
_____Business education		_____Gym
_____Home economics		_____Industrial arts
_____History		_____Civics
_____Math		_____Other

Extend Your Interest in Schoolwork

To become a better student you should increase your interest in all the subjects you study, and *particularly* in those you tend not to like. Remember: you can become interested in something—mathematics, civics, mountain climbing—whether you like it or not.

The best way to develop interest in a subject is to find out more about it. Find out what its content is, how it can help you become a better-educated person, and what it might contribute to your life. Another good way is to exert more effort in the subject. As you learn more about a subject and do better work in it, your interest is likely to grow.

If you increase your interest in a subject, you'll study it harder and longer—and with increasing enjoyment. And the chances are you will get better grades in it.

There Is Satisfaction in Studying Well

You learn any subject better if you get satisfaction from it. Your strongest satisfaction will come from the knowledge that *your* efforts have resulted in your gaining or improving a skill. You may be able to spell better, or write more interesting compositions. You may finally master that tough theorem in geometry.

On the other hand, the skill may be more practical. While you are learning to type, you may enjoy typing your English papers or your personal letters. In home economics or woodworking, you may obtain satisfaction from what you can do or make both at home and at school. Another kind of satisfaction comes from improved grades and better relations with parents and teachers.

Participate in Learning

Learning by doing is one of the best ways to learn. The more active your mind is, the more you learn and remember. Consider these two students in the same class:

Malcolm listens attentively. When the lecture is over, he can repeat almost word for word much of what the teacher said.

Margo listens attentively too. At the same time, she carries on a silent conversation with herself: "The teacher is talking about the importance of the West in American life...Uh-uh! Now *that* idea doesn't make sense to me!...That ties in nicely with what he said last week about greater democracy....I'll bet he'll say something about the effect of no more free land.... Sure enough, he did!"

It's clear that of the two, Margo is listening more attentively—participating more actively in the lecture. She related the new facts she was hearing to the facts she already knew. She analyzed, questioned, judged, anticipated. In her participation she learned much more than Malcolm did.

In other words, a poor learner is like an empty bottle into which the speaker pours facts like a liquid, or like a dry sponge soaking up information. A good learner thinks about and reacts to the information as it is presented.

Use What You Learn

The more you *use* what you're learning, the more effectively you'll learn it. You should continually seek opportunities to apply the knowledge and skills you are developing in your courses.

For example, suppose you want to boil potatoes more quickly. What should you do? Turn the fire higher? Put a tighter lid on the pot? Or what? From your general science course you *remember* that at normal atmospheric pressure, water boils at 212 degrees Fahrenheit. Therefore you *realize* that no matter how high you turn the flame, the water won't get hotter than 212 degrees. Then you *recall* that if you put a tighter lid on the pot, the pressure inside will increase. At increased atmospheric pressure, water boils at a temperature higher than 212 degrees. You tighten the lid, and the temperature inside the pot rises.

Suppose you are trying to mark off two identical pieces of lumber. From math and woodworking you recall how to measure two equal angles. You apply your knowledge and skill to perform this task.

From each such experience you learn new facts and ideas and use them to understand and deal with each new experience.

Practice Is Important...

You may learn one skill by practicing it only once. Another skill may have to be practiced again and again. In any case, the more frequently you practice a skill or study a fact, the more likely you are to remember it later when you need it.

Through practice you learn to spell more difficult words, to translate other languages into English, to recall important dates and events in history, to use a typewriter or play the piano.

Remember how, in lower grades, you had to learn the "times tables"—2×1 is 2, 2×2 is 4, and so on and on, until you knew all the tables automatically and instantly, without having to stop and think. In history, you repeated the names and dates of the first eight U.S. presidents until you could say them in your sleep. If you took a course in typing, you practiced over and over until you could type words, sentences, and paragraphs quickly and without errors.

...And So Is Review

Practice or repetition to keep from forgetting something you've already learned is *review*.

In grade school you learned the names and deeds of many early explorers of North America. You repeated those facts until you knew them well and could do well on a test about them. On the same test now, however, you would probably get a lower score. To do well, you would have to review the facts to fix them in your memory.

If you're studying another language, you learn new words every week. You may take a weekly quiz on them. Then, for the end-of-term exam, you have to review all the vocabulary words at once.

You should remember that if you review something just before you take a test on it, you probably will make a higher score. Similarly, if you review your part in a play just before the performance, you are more likely to say your lines correctly.

In fact, if you wish to remember anything or keep up your skill in something, you must review or use it again and again.

What Is a Learning Curve?

When you learn something, your learning follows a pattern, called the S-shaped curve. Such a curve appears in the graph following, for a student learning to type.

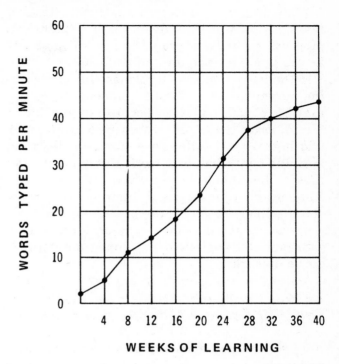

WEEKS OF LEARNING

Notice that the horizontal line at the bottom of the graph shows the number of weeks of practice—0, 4, 8, and so on. The vertical line shows the number of words per minute typed correctly—10, 20, and so on.

At the beginning of the forty-week training period the student increased his typing skill very slowly. After four weeks he could type only six correct words a minute. At the end of eight weeks he typed 12 words a minute; and at the end of twelve weeks, 14 words a minute. At this time the student's learning curve reached a so-called plateau, or level place. While he stayed on this level, he showed no improvement. However, he was learning to keep whole phrases in his mind rather than single words. This helped him improve his typing later.

From the end of the twelfth week to the end of the twenty-eighth week the student rapidly increased his rate of learning. In this period he raised his typing speed from 12 to 38 words a minute. After the twenty-eighth week, however, his learning curve reached another plateau—about 42 words a minute. At this time he was having much more difficulty going from 40 to 50 words a minute than he had earlier going from 30 to 40 words. In fact, he may have been getting close to his maximum typing ability—say, 50 words a minute.

Most people's learning patterns follow this S-shaped curve. In learning anything you usually progress slowly at first, then faster and faster. Next you slow down again. Again, you progress rapidly and then, finally, more slowly as you approach the limit of your ability.

If you have come to a level place in your learning curve, you should not feel discouraged. You may have such a plateau because of any one of a number of reasons. You may be learning new and higher-level skills. Or you may be learning new and better habits of work. But whatever the reason, you should keep up your interest in the subject and your efforts to improve. If you do, you are likely to get off the plateau and to start progressing again. Sooner or later, for instance, your new skills or habits may push your learning curve upward.

As You Learn, You Will Become More Accurate...

When you are learning anything, you may make many errors at first. As you continue to learn, however, you increase the percentage of your correct answers or reactions.

You can easily measure your accuracy in sports. In baseball, for example, you can keep track of your batting average by dividing the number of hits you make by the number of times you've been at bat. A ballplayer with a batting average of 300 thus has a batting *performance* of 30 percent. He performs well—gets a hit—30 percent of the time.

Suppose that during one baseball season you were at bat 60 times and made 10 hits. Your batting average was 10 divided by 60, or about 17 percent. If you raise your batting average to 25 percent during the next season, you greatly increase your accuracy—and become a much better player.

You can apply a similar index of accuracy to your schoolwork—math, science, history, English, and so on. As you learn you should gain in accuracy. If you continue to make mistakes, examine closely your learning methods, including your study skills and study habits. You might also ask your teacher for extra help.

...And You'll Be Faster...

In many subjects you can use speed as a measure of learning. You should figure speed in terms of the number of correct responses or reactions during a given unit of time.

In learning anything you can increase your speed in either of two ways: (1) by increasing the number of correct responses you make during a period of time, as you do in learning to type, or (2) by reducing the number of errors you make. Or you may do both.

As you learn typing, piano playing, or another language, for example, you make gains in knowledge, speed, and accuracy. Because of these gains, you also gain in speed. You type automatically, without thinking. You grow used to reading music and your hands respond immediately, striking the keys at the right times and in the right combinations. You learn a foreign vocabulary so that you can give the correct words instantly. In each of these areas you can determine your efficiency in terms of the number of correct responses.

...And Need Less Effort

If you have learned to operate a typewriter, you will remember your experiences. At first you used a great deal of effort. You pressed down one key and then another. You had to think about the letter and about the key that stood for that letter —and last, you had to think to press that key. You had to pay close attention, and when you made mistakes you were upset—and made even more. You found that typing was a terrific strain.

As you gained more skill, though, you found you had to make less and less effort. You pressed the keys automatically, without thinking about which key stood for which letter. You made fewer and fewer mistakes. Your fingers began to fly as they typed one word after another— rapidly, accurately, and easily.

This is also true of learning other skills. Remember when you first tried to play the piano, to roller-skate, to shoot a basketball through the hoop? Do you recall that when you started to learn those skills you had to use a lot of effort? Do you also recall that as you improved, you were able to cut down on the effort and begin to enjoy the activity?

Similarly, in learning English, history, science, or math you may have to use a lot of effort at first. As you get into the subject you find that you can study it with less and less conscious effort.

In the space following, list some skills you are learning in or out of school. Then indicate whether you are making more conscious effort or less than you did when you started to learn these skills.

Skill or subject	Amount of effort
1. _____	_____
2. _____	_____
3. _____	_____
4. _____	_____
5. _____	_____

Look at the Whole Problem

Once a man was lost in the wilderness. He wandered around helplessly because, as the saying goes, he couldn't see the forest for the trees. After a while he used his head as well as his feet. He hiked to the crest of the highest hill. There he climbed to the top of the tallest tree. As he looked around, he saw the forest. And he saw a stream that he could follow downhill to the nearest house.

Sometimes, after you've worked unsuccessfully on a problem for a long time, you suddenly see a way to solve it. Then you wonder, Why didn't I see that before?

Chances are that you failed to solve the problem earlier because you couldn't see the forest for the trees. When you finally saw the forest (problem) as a whole, you could understand how each tree (part) fitted in. Then you could understand and solve the problem.

This suggests that in studying any assignment —in English, history, science, or a foreign language—you should look at the assignment as a whole. If the assignment is a chapter to read, read the whole chapter quickly. Then read it carefully, part by part. Try to see how the parts fit together. Try to see the relationships between these parts and the chapter as a whole.

Learn Something in the Way You Will Use It

If you learn a fact or some other kind of information as you'll have to use it later, you'll learn it more quickly and more thoroughly. For example, if you're getting ready for a written test, prepare a list of important questions and write your answers as you would in taking such a test. If you're getting ready to give an oral report, prepare your outline and practice giving the report aloud as if you really were in front of the class. If you're learning to type business letters, practice typing an entire letter, not just isolated parts.

When you practice something in the way you will have to use it, you learn more effectively. It's like having a dress rehearsal the day before a play opens. Traditionally, the dress rehearsal is a mess—but the actual performance goes beautifully. Taking a tip from actors, make many of your study activities dress rehearsals for your performances before the class and teacher.

Use Techniques of Learning— Become a Better Student

To improve your schoolwork you can apply techniques of learning. You will learn best if you—

• are interested in your subjects of study and have definite goals;
• get a feeling of satisfaction from learning;
• are active, mentally or physically, in what you are studying or doing;
• remember that the more *often* you practice a skill, the more likely you are to learn it;
• expect very slow progress at first, then faster and faster progress;
• look at an assignment as a whole before studying the parts;
• learn your material in the way you will use it.

More Things to Do

1. List your school subjects in order of interest, placing the one in which you are most interested highest on the list, and so on down the line.

2. Choose a current reading assignment. Divide it in half. Read the first half the night before class. Read the second half in the morning before class. Which part of the assignment did you remember best? What does this suggest?

3. Divide another assignment in half. Read the first part once. Read the second part three or four times. Which part did you remember best? What does this suggest?

3•How can you improve your memory and understanding?

"I read this chapter twice and I don't remember a word of it," Linda complains. "Studying is a waste of time." Obviously, for Linda such studying *is* a waste. Is this your story too? If so, read on!

You Can Develop Your Memory

First, keep in mind that there are two main kinds of memory. One is *routine* memory; the other is *reasoning* memory.

In routine memory work you repeat something again and again until you can recall it mechanically—word for word as you learned it. Like a parrot, you may be able to repeat what you learned without understanding it.

Whether or not you completely understand what you're memorizing, you frequently need this mechanical or automatic kind of memory. In math you must memorize number combinations so that you can use them instantly and without error. In learning a foreign language you must memorize vocabulary so that you can translate correctly. In science you must memorize certain formulas so that you can apply them in experiments. In history you must memorize certain important dates, names, and events. In English you sometimes must memorize a poem or part of a play.

In reasoning (or rational) memory work, you try to understand and think about what you're reading or hearing. Later you may not be able to repeat word for word what you learned, but you are able to describe, explain, discuss, or apply it intelligently in your own words or in your own way.

You must often employ this kind of memory in studying. For example, you use rational memory in math to solve a reasoning problem; in English, to explain the meaning of a short story, a poem, or a play; in science, to describe how hydrogen gas is made; and in history, to outline the main international developments since World War II.

If you want to recall later what you're studying, use the kind of remembering that is best suited to what you are learning and to the purpose of this learning. You remember the alphabet automatically when you use a dictionary or the index of an encyclopedia. If it is necessary that you understand the principal characteristics of O. Henry's short stories in order to discuss them in class, you use reasoning memory.

Sometimes you must use reasoning memory and routine memory together. For example, you have to remember the multiplication tables automatically to solve a reasoning problem in math. You also need routine memory to recall exactly certain highlights in the background of Thomas Jefferson that explain his contributions to the Declaration of Independence.

Although one can't draw a hard-and-fast line between these two kinds of memory, each of them will be considered separately in this chapter.

Remembering Automatically

Tips for improving routine memory:

1. Consider *why* you're memorizing something. Be sure you understand the meaning or the use of the material you're studying. If you

think about the reason for memorizing something, you'll learn it faster and better and remember it longer.

2. As you memorize something, *test* yourself on it. Do this again and again until you can say it or write it correctly and automatically without stopping to think. Then check yourself. If you made a mistake, test yourself again until you've written it correctly.

3. *Review* what you've memorized. Later the same day or at the end of the week, test yourself again. If you make mistakes, practice until you're correct every time.

Check Your Ability to Memorize Different Materials

Which kinds of materials are easiest to memorize? To find out, try this experiment:

1. For one minute, work on memorizing the twenty nonsense syllables that follow. Then close your book. Write down as many of these syllables as you can recall. Check your list with the original list. How many did you remember correctly? _____

Nonsense syllables: cag, luz, rov, bex, paz, yem, zoy, kaz, buw, mib, voc, cem, ral, niy, nok, yeb, cuw, der, yib, zar.

2. For one minute, work at memorizing the twenty partly related words that follow. Then close your book, write down those you can remember, and check yourself. How many did you recall this time? _____

Related words: horse, cab, wheel, driver, car, road, hurt, nurse, doctor, water, bed, rest, pen, ink, paper, word, teacher, pupil, parent, home.

3. For one minute, work at memorizing the sentence that follows. Then write it down and check it with the original. How many words did you recall correctly? _____

Sentence: John Miller, who talked with his teacher today, said that he plans to attend a medical school to learn surgery.

Compare your recall scores on the three kinds of material. On which did you get the highest score? _____ On which the lowest score? _____ Which kind of material is easiest to remember? _____ Why? _____

Use the "Whole" Method of Learning

In the experiment above, you probably scored highest in the last part—the section that you could memorize as a whole rather than as more or less separate, meaningless parts. Try learning things as "wholes" in your schoolwork, too. You'll find it works wonders. For example, if you are to memorize an entire poem, memorize it as a whole from beginning to end, not part by part or line by line.

In the "whole" method you get a broad outline of what you are learning. You are likely to see all the parts and the relationships between them. In the "part" method you may see only one part or only a few parts, but not the whole.

In part-by-part learning, moreover, you probably will spend much more time on the first part than on the other parts. You learn the first part of a poem because you practice that part again and again. You start out and go on until you make a mistake. Then you go back to the beginning and start over again.

In the meantime, what about the parts at the end? You may hardly get a chance to practice *them!* If you use the "whole" method, however, you'll be distributing your attention equally among all the parts.

To compare the methods of learning, make an experiment with the beautiful lines below. They are from the prose works of John Donne, an English poet who lived from 1573 to 1631.

First, read the entire statement. Think about it. What does it say to you? Its message probably is even more important today than it was when it was written hundreds of years ago. An understanding of that message will help you as you memorize it. This is true of anything you try to memorize.

Try first to memorize the lines by the "part" method—line by line. If that method doesn't seem to work for you, try the "whole" method:

No man is an island, entire of itself;
every man is a piece of the continent, a part of the main;
if a clod be washed away by the sea, Europe is the less,
as well as if a promontory were,
as well as if a manor of thy friends or of thine own were;
any man's death diminishes me,
because I am involved in mankind;
and therefore never send to know
    for whom the bell tolls;
it tolls for thee.

Which method worked better for you—the part method or the whole? _____

Why? _____

_____

Index Cards Help You Learn and Remember

Using 3×5 index cards can help you become a better student. You might use them in starting to learn the vocabulary of another language. Let's assume you're starting to study Spanish.

On one side of a card write a Spanish word. On the other side write its meaning in English.

After you've filled out twenty-five cards with different words, start to practice with them:

1. Place all the cards in a pile with the Spanish words showing.

2. Look at the Spanish word on the first card. Give the English word and then check yourself by looking at the back of the card.

3. If you gave the correct English word, place the card in a "do know" pile. If you didn't, put it in a "don't know" pile. Repeat this for each card.

4. After you've tested yourself on the Spanish words on all twenty-five cards, shuffle the cards in the "don't know" pile. Again, test and check yourself on each word on these cards. Repeat until *all* the cards are in the "do know" pile.

5. Carry the word cards with you. Later the same day or on the next day, test and check yourself on all twenty-five of the word cards.

For each Spanish lesson in your book, make up new word cards. Some of the cards should have phrases or short sentences instead of single words. You can use the same cards to learn to translate the English words into Spanish. Just turn them over so that the English words show.

Every Friday review the word cards you have made for the week just ending. You should be able to give the English or Spanish equivalent of each word, phrase, or sentence quickly and correctly. Also on Friday, review words from previous weeks that still give you trouble.

Sometimes you'll want to *write* the equivalent word instead of saying it. This will help you learn how to spell correctly and is very important in preparing for a written test. Remember that the best way to learn something is to learn it in the way you are going to use it.

You can also use this card method to learn new English words. On one side of a card write the word; on the other side, the meaning or meanings of that word after you've looked it up in your dictionary.

Again, you can use such cards to learn place names such as capitals of states or countries.

Memory Crutches: Yes or No?

Some people use crutches, or special aids, to remember facts and figures. These may be catchwords, jingles, or formulas.

A familiar catchword and a crutch sentence help music students learn what letters the notes in the spaces and on the lines in the treble clef stand for. Starting from the bottom of the clef, the letters in the four spaces are F, A, C, E: *face.* That's easy to remember. Also starting from the bottom of the clef, the letters on the five lines are E, G, B, D, F. You can remember these letters if you memorize the sentence *Every Good Boy Does Fine.*

The memory crutch most often used in the United States probably is

"In fourteen hundred and ninety-two Columbus sailed the ocean blue."

A schoolteacher once admitted she had always had trouble with the spelling of *principal* and *principle.* She composed two sentences to help her remember which spelling was called for: "The princi*pal* is my *pal.* He is a man of high princi*ples.*"

In using crutches such as these, keep in mind that they can be good temporary devices for remembering certain facts and figures. As soon as you know a fact or figure very well, you no longer need the crutch; it simply turns into useless clutter in your mind. Crutches are not a substitute for practice and review.

A good rule to follow: *Use a memory crutch only if it really helps you recall something, and throw it away as soon as you can do without it.*

Write It Down

One of the best ways to remember something is to write it down. That is why businessmen have appointment books and why people carry shopping lists when they go to the store. It is why students take notes during a lecture or a club meeting. They use the notes later to report or to summarize what was said or done.

If you've made notes on something important that you've read or heard, you can quickly and easily refer to them to refresh your memory. You won't have to worry about forgetting. In fact, you'll free your mind to think about other things.

Say It Aloud

If you are assigned to make an oral report in class, practice saying it aloud to yourself at home. Listening to yourself will help you remember what you plan to say. If you have a part in a school play, it will help you learn your lines if you practice speaking them aloud until you really know them by heart. If a friend or relative will listen and correct you, all the better.

Remembering with Understanding

Although some things must be memorized mechanically, reasoning or understanding is needed to learn others.

To understand anything, as we have seen, you must see the whole, the parts, and the relationships between those parts. For instance, consider this math problem:

A refrigerator car is loaded with tubs of butter. Each tub weighs 60 pounds. The butter will sell at the store for 90 cents a pound. The car holds 480 tubs. What is the total dollar value of the carload of butter?

To solve this problem you must recognize and remember each of its important details and then relate each detail to all the other details. Specifically, after reading and thinking about the problem, you decide you must first figure out the worth of one tub of butter. You multiply the number of pounds (60) by the price per pound (90¢). The answer: $54 a tub. Next, you must figure out the dollar worth of the entire carload, so you multiply the price per tub ($54) by the number of tubs (480). Total worth: $25,920.

In science, too, you must see the relationships between ideas to understand how something works—an electric doorbell, for example:

1. When you push the button of the doorbell, you make an electrical connection. This allows current to flow from a battery or other source of electric power through the doorbell.

2. In the doorbell the electric current flows through the wire of an electromagnet. The electromagnet is an iron core with a coil of wire wrapped around it.

3. As electricity flows through the bell's electromagnet, the magnet sets up lines of force that attract the clapper of the bell. The clapper strikes the bell and makes a ringing noise.

4. At the instant the clapper hits the bell, the electric current is automatically shut off and the clapper springs back, away from the bell.

5. When the clapper is farthest from the bell, it connects the electrical current. This causes the electromagnet to attract the clapper again— and the bell rings once more.

As you can easily see, you'll have to *understand* this series of events in order to remember it for any length of time!

More Suggestions about Understanding and Remembering

If you look for the main ideas and see the relationships between them, you're more likely to understand and remember what you read, see, and hear. Such ideas—vital to comprehending a subject—are generally easier to remember than detailed facts or figures.

Here are steps that will help you spot the main ideas and details of a chapter in a textbook or reference book:

1. *Skim the chapter.* Reading the chapter as a whole will help you understand its parts better. You'll find the keys to these parts in the headings within each chapter.

2. *Carefully study the first part of the chapter.*

   a) Change the heading of this part into a question. If the heading is "Causes of the Civil War," mentally change it to "What were the causes of the Civil War?"

   b) Read to get the answer. As you read this

part of the chapter, look for the answers and make written notes on them.

c) Repeat the answers to yourself in your own words as soon as you finish reading. If some points are not clear, go back and reread.

3. *Go on to the next part.* Again change the heading into a question. Then read to get the answer to your question.

4. *Summarize the chapter.* In your own words write a brief summary in outline form. Give the major points and important details, but leave out minor details and anecdotes used for illustration. In writing this summary, you'll discover which parts of the chapter you understand and which parts need further study.

Plan Your Study

1. Approach each subject determined to remember and understand it. Ask yourself questions about it. Don't let your mind wander.

2. As you read a chapter in a subject such as history or science, study the parts in the order in which they appear. In each of these subjects, ideas are usually developed gradually—first idea A, then idea B. To understand B, you must first understand A. If you read an entire chapter during a single study period, you'll be better able to see the relationships between the ideas presented in it.

3. As you study a chapter, try to understand all the main ideas. If you don't, you may have trouble understanding the main ideas in the chapters that follow. Master each chapter before you go on to the next.

4. Talk to your teacher at once if you feel that you're getting behind in your work or failing to understand the subject. He will be glad to give you more help—during class or after school. He may also find a classmate to help you.

More Study Planning

1. Make home study periods *long* enough. If you study for only a few minutes at a time, you don't give yourself time to warm up and really get into the material. In fact, you may just waste the time.

2. Make home study periods *short* enough. Otherwise you'll become tired or bored and remember little of what you studied. What is "long enough" and "short enough" for *you*? Try studying a subject such as history or science for about forty minutes at a time; then lengthen or shorten the period according to your needs.

3. In memorizing routinely—words in a foreign vocabulary, for instance—study for a period of only fifteen to thirty minutes. Then do something else.

4. If you're studying new material in a subject, you probably should have regular study periods—say a half hour a day five days a week. If you're reviewing old material, do this during a special study period ranging from a half hour to an hour or more once a week.

Review . . . and Review

To remember and understand a subject best, review it in several study periods. In the first study period learn a number of important facts. In the second period, perhaps a day later, review these facts. This strengthens your understanding and memory of the new material. At the third study period, perhaps a week after the second, review the material again.

Good written notes or outlines will help you review the material quickly. If you recite to yourself and correct errors in each study or review period, you can find your weak spots and eliminate them. Then you'll understand and remember the reviewed material better and will require less time for reviewing.

How long do you remember the material you study? According to scientific experiments, you quickly forget most of what you learn. What can you do? To retain what you learn, study the material *beyond* the point at which you can just barely recall it. You must *overlearn*. If you learn words in another language more easily by writing them down, write each one twenty times or more—not three or four times.

Because review is so important in learning, it is sometimes called "the mother of studies."

Tips on Remembering and Understanding

1. Remember the *important* things. If you forget small details, don't worry.

2. Understand the *meaning* of what you're studying so that you will be more likely to remember it.

3. In general, learn by the *"whole" method* rather than part by part. You can combine the two methods whenever the material you're studying seems to call for it.

4. Fit the *period of study* to the kind of material you're studying.

5. *Practice* correct skills and responses. Check yourself. Practicing something the wrong way over and over won't help you a bit!

6. *Review* often.

7. Use memory *crutches* sparingly. They may be more of a hindrance than a help. If you don't need such crutches, don't use them.

8. Put real, honest-to-goodness *effort* into each subject you study. This will help you develop an interest in the subject—and thus enjoy it more.

9. *Repeat* aloud to yourself.

10. *Overlearn* material you want to remember.

11. Learn actively. *Think* about what you're reading or hearing. This will help you remember.

More Things to Do

1. Choose two chapters in one of your textbooks. Study one by the "part" method, the other by the "whole" method. Which method helped you understand and remember the material better? Why?

2. Get a pack of 3×5 index cards. Select ten words that you have trouble spelling and write each word on a card. Review them once a day for a week. Can you spell them any better now?

3. Test yourself on the ten books you've most recently read. Can you remember the plot—in broad outline—of each? Make an index card for each one you miss; then review. Retest yourself. (Keeping a card for each book you read will help you get started on book reports, too.)

4•ON YOUR MARK, GET SET-STUDY!

Laurie is getting set to study. Sitting on her bed, she opens her history textbook to chapter 3, "Early New England Settlers." Then she turns on the radio and picks up her hairbrush. She reads: "The first permanent English settlement in New England was the Pilgrim town of Plymouth, Massachusetts. The Pilgrims landed ...(*brush, brush*)... at what became Plymouth ...(*great beat to that song!*)...in 1620... (*brush*)...after a long...(*hair as long as mine really needs two hundred strokes a day*)... and terrifying ocean voyage..."

You can imagine how much Laurie is learning about the Pilgrims! Now consider her classmate Michael. When he's ready to study, he goes to a quiet room and sits down at a desk or table. He gets his books and other materials together and organized, and reads or writes his assignment in a systematic way.

There are many different ways to get ready to study. The best ways, like the one Michael uses, have a number of things in common. Some are discussed in this chapter.

Make a Study Plan

To study effectively, develop a definite study plan and then carry it out.

First, try to build good attitudes toward your studies. To do this, consider *why* you are studying each subject and each assignment. Ask yourself, What can this subject teach me about my world—and myself?

If you look at a subject as something you're forced to study whether you like it or not, you'll naturally dislike it. If you think of a subject as a challenge, you'll develop an interest in it.

Second, build good study habits. One of the most important study habits is starting work promptly on the job to be done. A poor "studier" postpones working on an assignment. He may complete it only a few minutes before—or even after—it is due. A student with good study habits starts work as soon as possible and completes the assignment in plenty of time.

Third, make and keep a study schedule. Such a schedule will help you study all your subjects as systematically as possible.

How to Make a Study Schedule

How can you learn to prepare a study schedule? By actually doing it! Plan your schedule for one week, using the form on page 24 as an example. Then do your best to keep this schedule for the whole week.

You probably should plan one study period a day, five days a week, for each subject you are taking, as shown in the schedule. Suppose you have a study period from 9 to 9:45 A.M. on Monday. During that time you might plan to study math. Make the appropriate entry: "9:00–9:45 A.M. Math." This entry appears in the example in the schedule on page 24.

If you have two study periods at school, you can use them to complete assignments in two subjects—math and social studies. If you have only one study period at school, it may be necessary to provide for more study periods at home to complete all your assignments.

MY SCHEDULE OF STUDY PERIODS FOR THE WEEK: _____ TO _____

Example MON	SUN	MON	TUES	WED	THURS	FRI	SAT
9:00 9:45 AM Math.							
1:00 1:45 PM S.S.							
7:30 8:10 PM Eng.							
8:30 9:00 PM Sci.							

Key: Eng.—English; Sci.—Science; Math.—Mathematics; S.S.—Social Studies

In making up your schedule, plan to study *first* the subject you find most difficult and dull. This is when you feel relatively fresh, not when you're tired. Leave the subject you find easiest and most interesting for the last.

The real test—sticking to it—comes after you've filled in your study schedule for a week. Try it out for a week. Were there problems? Did you allow too little time for some subjects, too much for others? Can you improve the schedule? At the end of the week prepare another schedule for the week to come. In making this schedule draw on your experience during the first week. If you make and revise your schedules over a month, you can develop a weekly schedule that meets nearly all your study needs. Keep in mind that you may have certain *long-term* projects that require extra study time, and that you may have to plan study time to prepare for tests.

Where's the Right Place to Study?

Whether you're at home or at school, try to find a quiet place for study. At school a study hall or the library may be best. At home it may be your bedroom or a corner of the living room or dining room.

It helps if the temperature is comfortable— about 70 degrees Fahrenheit. If the room is too hot, you'll become sleepy; if it's too cold, you'll think more about how uncomfortable you are than about what you're studying.

Check the lighting. Indirect lighting is easier on your eyes than direct lighting. Uniform lighting over a textbook page or work surface is better than uneven lighting. Natural daylight—but not direct sunlight—is best of all.

Sit in a straight-backed chair at a desk or table. Although an armchair can be more comfortable, it can also put you to sleep. Using the same chair in the same room each time you study helps you get into a studying mood more quickly.

Because your studying depends so much on reading, you should be sure your eyesight is good. Eyes should be tested at least once every two years. If, after ten or fifteen minutes of reading, your head aches or your eyes smart, burn, or feel tired, you should go to an eye specialist.

Fatigue, illness, hunger, or thirst can keep you from doing a good job of studying. Be careful, though, not to use these conditions as excuses to escape studying or delay it longer than necessary.

Have Study Aids on Hand

In getting ready to study, have at hand all the study aids you'll need—pencils, pens, paper, and the special tools, textbooks, and reference materials needed for specific subjects.

Read the items listed below and check each one Yes or No to indicate which study aids you have and which ones you do not have.

	Yes	No		Yes	No
1. Textbooks	___	___	8. Pencil, eraser	___	___
2. Workbooks	___	___	9. Pen	___	___
3. Notebook	___	___	10. Paper clips	___	___
4. Reference books	___	___	11. Ruler	___	___
5. Dictionary	___	___	12. Calendar	___	___
6. Thesaurus	___	___	13. Watch or clock	___	___
7. Paper	___	___			

Keep an Assignment Book

A good student always writes down his assignments. Then he doesn't have to trust his memory; he has a written record he can readily consult. He can tell at a glance exactly what he must do and when he must do it.

It's a good idea to keep a small assignment notebook that you can carry easily to school, the library, your home, or wherever you need it.

Carefully enter your assignment for each of your subjects in this notebook. While you're in class, make certain that you have heard, read, or copied the assignment correctly. When you get ready to do the assignment, read carefully what you've written in your notebook.

Have Large Notebooks

To study your assignments, you should have one or more large notebooks—either spiral-bound or loose-leaf. Each should hold sheets of paper approximately 8½ × 11 inches in size.

You may have one notebook for each subject or one for all your subjects. If you have one notebook for all subjects, cardboard dividers or plastic tabs will help you keep the subjects separate. You can buy notebooks, paper fillers, and dividers in most bookstores and stationery stores.

Arrange your class notes and your homework assignments in the notebook according to the

dates on which you wrote them. Do this for each subject you're taking. In English, however, you may prefer to arrange the notes according to fields—for instance, literature, vocabulary, spelling, and language usage.

From time to time, perhaps once a month, do a "notebook cleaning." Go through the notebook and take out the pages of notes you no longer need. You may want to store these pages in large envelopes for possible future use.

Removing pages of old and useless notes from your notebook will help you keep it in good order and make it easier to find what you want.

Have Different Kinds of Paper

You'll need different kinds of paper, usually letterhead size (8½ × 11), for different purposes. You should have the following on hand:

- Ruled paper for compositions, tests, and the like
- Unruled paper for drawings
- Scratch paper for rough notes and for drafts of compositions
- Typing paper (if you use a typewriter)

Avoid Distractions

To get the most from studying, you must *concentrate*. This means avoiding or removing distractions. Any distraction is bound to cut down on study efficiency.

Even a superstudent can't do two things well at the same time. In other words, if you're studying don't try to listen to a radio or TV program—or brush your hair—at the same time. If you do, not only will your homework assignment suffer, but you'll spend more time on it than is really necessary.

It's best to study in a room by yourself. Keep the door of the room closed and ask others to stay away until you've finished. If you don't have a room to yourself, find a desk or table away from others so that you can concentrate.

Before you start to study, clear your desk or table of such distracting materials as photos, magazines, souvenirs, and letters. These things tend to interfere with studying. Instead, have at hand all the aids and supplies you need to do your assignments.

Don't daydream. If you let your mind wander to the date you had last night, to tomorrow's football game, or to the success you'll be after graduation, you can't do your assignments efficiently.

Take a Break

During a fairly long period of study—an hour or more—look up from your work for a second or two every now and then. In addition, take a break and relax at the end of every half hour to an hour of study. Decide *before* you begin to study when you'll take your break.

A word of warning on this business of relaxing: Don't make the break too long. If you do, you'll lose your study pace. Don't make it too short, either, or it won't refresh you. Don't take so many breaks that you spend more time relaxing than studying. A good break is three to five minutes.

During a study break get up and stretch. Walk around; get something to eat or drink. Speak to the family. Then go back to studying.

Check Yourself on Getting Ready to Study

Read each statement. To indicate your answer, mark a check under Yes or No.

	Yes	No
1. I try to become interested in my subjects of study.	——	——
2. I feel that most of my courses are worth studying.	——	——
3. I do my study assignments on time or before they are due.	——	——
4. I can concentrate on the study work at hand.	——	——
5. I try to study in a quiet place.	——	——
6. I keep the radio and TV turned off when I study.	——	——

	Yes	No
7. While studying, I discourage interruptions such as family conversations and telephone calls.	——	——
8. I usually study my hardest subject first.	——	——
9. I try to finish an assignment before leaving it.	——	——
10. I have and follow a study plan and a time schedule.	——	——
11. I have arranged good physical conditions for study.	——	——
12. I usually study in the same place each day.	——	——
13. I usually keep my desk clear of unnecessary and distracting materials.	——	——
14. I usually take only a few short breaks when I study.	——	——
15. I usually have the necessary books, supplies, and other study materials at hand.	——	——

More Things to Do

1. Make a schedule of your study periods for the coming week. Indicate the hour of the day and the subject to be studied at that time. Do your best to keep to this schedule.

2. Make a written list of the things that still disturb you when you study. For each of these, figure out what you might do about it.

3. Make a list of the books, tools, and materials you should have ready for study of history, mathematics, or English. Compare your list with the lists made by other students.

5 • how well do you read?

If you can read well, many things in your everyday life will be made easier for you. It will be easier to qualify for a driver's license or to fill out a good application for a job. It will be easier to enjoy an interesting book or to follow written instructions on how to put together a stereo set.

Why Read Better?

Here are some reasons:

1. If you learn to read better, you probably will do better work in school. About 90 percent of all your study activities at school and at home require reading. Good students are usually better readers than poor students. This was found to be true in a study of high school juniors of about the same intelligence.

2. Generally, the better reader you are, the more job opportunities you'll have. As an employee rises in a company, he must do more reading and do it more effectively. A number of businesses have organized reading-improvement courses. Such courses have helped company executives and supervisors increase their reading efficiency by about 25 percent. By learning to read better in school, you can prepare yourself for a job and for job advancement after you leave school.

Are You a Good Reader?

If you're a good reader, you recognize words and phrases quickly and correctly. You have a large vocabulary. You readily understand what you read. You have different reading speeds for different purposes.

To understand what you read, you may use one or more of the following reading skills:

1. *Find the main idea* of a reading passage — a short story, for example — and summarize it in a few sentences.

2. *Find the ideas that support* or explain the main idea.

3. *Follow any directions* that may be given.

4. *Draw correct conclusions* or generalizations from what you read.

5. *Judge the purpose* of the author in writing the passage.

If you want to become a better reader, you must have the will to improve your reading skills and *you must know how to do so.* Here are some ways:

Reading Skill 1: Follow Directions

Directions for doing or making something must be read carefully and followed exactly. In this kind of reading you generally read and then reread a paragraph. You may read a sentence, do as it says, and then read the sentence again to check on whether you did it correctly.

To give yourself practice in reading directions, read and carry out the instructions that follow.

HOW TO DETERMINE YOUR READING SPEED

One of the best ways to improve your reading is to develop faster reading rates. To do this you must know exactly how to figure out your own reading rate—that is, the number of words you read per minute.

To keep track of your reading time and to determine your reading rate, use the last column of the time record shown below. You will need a watch with a second hand. You will also need a story or article to read. When you're ready, take the following steps:

1. Write down the *exact time* you started reading the story or article. The example below is for a reader whose starting time was exactly 12 minutes past the hour.

Time Record

	Example	Your time
Starting time	12:00	
Finishing time	13:20	
Reading time	1:20	
Reading rate	187.5	

2. Read the story as quickly as you can, but be sure you *understand* what you read.

3. Write down your finishing time. The example shows a finishing time of 13 minutes and 20 seconds past the hour.

4. Figure out your reading time. From your finishing time, subtract your starting time. In the example the difference is 1:20—one minute and 20 seconds. Write your difference to the right of the "Reading time" example.

5. Now figure out your reading rate. Change your reading time into your reading rate. This is how to do it:

a) Count the number of words in the story you have just read. (Don't count *a, an, and,* or *the.*) Suppose the number of words is 250.

b) Change your reading time from minutes and seconds into seconds. In the example, 1:20 equals 60 seconds (one minute) plus 20 seconds—a total of 80 seconds.

c) Divide the number of words in the story by the number of seconds in your reading time. For instance, 250 divided by 80 equals 3.125—the number of words you read per second.

d) Multiply the number of words per second by 60 to obtain the number of words per minute. In the example, the number 3.125 multiplied by 60 equals 187.5—the number of words per minute.

e) To give yourself practice figuring out reading rates, solve this problem: If you read a 1350-word story in 3 minutes and 45 seconds, what was your reading rate (the number of words read per minute)? The answer is 360.

Reading Skill 2: Adapt Your Reading Rate to Your Purpose and Material

A poor reader has only one reading rate—slow. He uses the same rate in reading everything from a textbook chapter to a daily newspaper to a comic book.

If you're a good reader, you have different reading rates—a rate for each reading purpose and for each kind of reading material.

First, adapt your rate to your *purpose*. If your purpose in reading a textbook chapter is to find out in general what's in it, skim the chapter quickly. If your purpose is to remember the main points in the chapter in preparation for a test, read the chapter more slowly, perhaps writing down these points.

Second, adapt your rate to your *material*. If you're reading a story in a popular magazine, read at a very rapid rate. If you're reading a textbook chapter, read at a slower rate.

You don't read all your textbooks at the same rate, either. You probably read social studies at a faster rate than you read a textbook for science, math, or a foreign language. Generally, you read a story or a description at a faster rate than you read a problem or an explanation.

Whatever your reading purpose or material, you can almost certainly increase your reading rates. One way to do this is to *force* yourself to read somewhat faster than you usually do, and to avoid looking back at what you've just read. If you try to read faster, you'll have to concentrate on the material more closely and will probably understand it better.

AN EXERCISE TO INCREASE YOUR READING RATE

First, following the steps just described, determine your present reading rate.

Write down your starting time. Then read the following article as fast as you can, making certain you *understand* what you're reading. After you finish the article, you'll take a short quiz on it.

HOW DO YOUR EYES BEHAVE?

If you are like most persons, you have only a general idea of what your eyes are doing when you read. You know, of course, that your eyes move from left to right along a line of print. This eye movement is called the *forward sweep*. You also know that they move quickly from the right end of one line to the left end of the line just below it. This eye movement is called the *return sweep*.

You may believe that your eyes move smoothly and steadily along a line of type and that in doing so they are reading words. In reality, your eyes do not behave that way. Instead, they move along a line in stop-go-stop-go movements. When your eyes stop or *pause* for a small fraction of a second, they are picking up groups of words and are transmitting these words to your brain. Your brain, of course, provides the meanings for these words. While your eyes are moving, you are not getting meanings from the printed words. Only when your eyes pause do you get these meanings.

You may think that, while reading, your eyes focus on the first word, then on the second word, then on the third word, and so on in each line. If your eyes focus, or fixate, for an instant on each word in a line, you are a very slow reader.

Also you probably have trouble understanding what you read. If you are a good or superior reader, your eyes fixate on one word but at the same time pick up one or two words on either side. That is, your *eye span* is made up of three to five words. The better reader you are, the fewer your eye pauses and the wider your eye span.

You may also believe that, if you are an efficient reader, your eyes often go back and reread —usually for more thorough understanding. As a matter of fact, however, if you are a superior reader, your eyes seldom return to a word they have already seen in the same line or in a preceding line. When your eyes do reread, this is called an *eye regression*. Such a regression can interfere with your understanding of what you read. For this reason the good reader has few or no eye regressions while he is reading.

Again, you may believe that moving your lips, tongue, and throat muscles all help your eyes to see words, and your brain to give them meanings. This is not true. If you say words aloud or you pronounce them softly, using your lips and your other muscles of speech, you definitely slow down your silent reading.

You can read words much faster with your eyes than with your lips. Therefore, when the good reader reads silently, he uses his eyes to pick up groups of words. At the same time he tries not to pronounce words either aloud or to himself. In reading silently, he tries to get rid of the oral reading habits he developed when he was learning to read.

Because you can move your eyes much faster than you can move your head or your finger, you should not turn your head while reading or point with your finger. These, too, are reading habits that slow down your silent reading.

If your eyes don't help you read as efficiently as you would like to, what can you do? According to psychologists, poor eye movements seem to be more a result of poor reading habits than a cause of such habits. Therefore, if you wish to improve your eye movements in silent reading, you should work to read more rapidly. Concentrate more on what you are reading. Try to get meanings accurately and completely from the printed page.

As soon as you finish the article, write down your finishing time. Then compute your reading time and rate. The article has 600 words.

Next, take the following true-false test. Read

the first statement. If this statement is true, mark + on the line at the left. If it is false, mark 0 on the line at the left. Do the same for each of the other statements.

A COMPREHENSION TEST ON "How Do Your Eyes Behave?"

_____ 1. If you are a good reader, your eyes sweep along a line of print without stopping.

_____ 2. You get the meaning of a word or word group only while your eyes are pausing.

_____ 3. To improve your reading, focus your eyes quickly on every word in a line of print.

_____ 4. The narrower your eye span, the better your reading.

_____ 5. The shorter your eye pause, the better your reading.

_____ 6. By rereading words and word groups, you improve your reading efficiency.

_____ 7. In silent reading you should not move your lips, tongue, or throat muscles.

_____ 8. You can read much faster silently than orally.

_____ 9. In reading, as in magic, "the hand is quicker than the eye."

_____10. Poor eye movements appear to be more a result than a cause of poor reading habits.

(Answers are at the end of this chapter.)

Reading Skill 3: Reading Word Groups

As the article "How Do Your Eyes Behave?" pointed out, you should *not* read like this:

"The
    time
       has
          come,"
            the
               Walrus
                  said,

Rather, you should read word group by word group, like this:

"To talk of many things:
Of shoes—and ships—and sealing wax—
Of cabbages—and kings—
And why the sea is boiling hot—
And whether pigs have wings."*

_____
*From *Through the Looking Glass,* by Lewis Carroll.

Make a Reading-Improvement Plan

If you work out a better-reading plan, you may increase your reading rates for many different purposes and for many kinds of materials. You may also improve your understanding of these materials.

By working on better reading systematically day by day, you may reach and even pass such goals as these:

• 350 words a minute—reading a story or novel for enjoyment
• 250 words a minute—reading a textbook chapter
• 200 words a minute—reading detailed or complex instructions

You may want to include the following procedures in your reading-improvement plan:

1. Set aside 15 to 30 minutes every day for reading practice. If possible, read at the same hour and in the same place each time.

2. Choose a book that is interesting and fairly easy to read—a novel, perhaps.

3. For your first practice, read chapter I of the book. Keep track of this reading by filling in figure 4, "Record of My Reading Practices." Write down your starting time. Read the chapter somewhat faster than usual. Then write down your finishing time. Next compute your reading time and your reading rate—the number of words you read per minute.

a) To find your reading rate, determine the number of words in an average line of the book. Count the number of words in each of five typical lines. Suppose these numbers are 11, 9, 12,

10, and 9 words. Add these numbers: the total is 51. Divide the total by five: the average number of words per line is 10.2.

b) Count the number of lines you read. Suppose this number is 600 lines. Then find the total number of words you read. At 10.2 words a line, you read a total of 6120 words.

c) Compute your reading rate. Divide the number of words you read by the number of minutes you read. Suppose you read for 30 minutes. Divide 6120 by 30—this equals 204, the number of words you read a minute. This is your reading rate.

d) Enter your reading rate in figure 5, "My Reading Rate Graph."

4. For your second practice, read chapter 2. Take the same steps you took during your first practice.

5. Read through each chapter of the book in turn. Have someone ask you questions about the chapter you just read. Enter the figures called for in figure 5. Keep trying to increase your reading rate for each chapter.

Increase Your Vocabulary

Your reading abilities depend a great deal on the words you know. In general, the larger your vocabulary, the better reader you are. If your vocabulary is small, you are more likely to stumble over the difficult words. You may even fail to understand the meaning of the sentence you read.

To increase your reading vocabulary, learn as many new words as you can. As a starter, write down and learn the meanings of three new words each day. If you do this for a year, you'll add about 1100 words to your vocabulary! Actually, this is not a particularly large number of words to learn. The average high school freshman already has a vocabulary of about 35,000 words.

In working to improve your vocabulary, keep in mind that many words have two or more meanings. Take the word *dusted*. In the sentence *The girl dusted the table*, the word *dusted* means "cleaned." In the sentence *The woman dusted the doughnuts with powdered sugar*, the word means "sprinkled."

If a word has such different meanings, how do you know which is the right meaning in a particular case? You can tell which meaning applies by reading the context—the sentence in which the word appears.

To learn the meaning of an unfamiliar word, look it up in your dictionary. When you find it, read each of the meanings given. Select the meaning that best fits the context in which the word is used. If you come across a new word in a textbook, you may find its definition in that chapter or elsewhere in the book—perhaps in a glossary near the back of the book. Increasing your vocabulary in these ways will help you become a better reader.

Understanding What You Read

Whether you read quickly or slowly, whether you have a large or a small vocabulary, you must understand what you read. This requires several different reading abilities. For instance, can you find the main idea and the supporting ideas in a paragraph? Can you draw correct conclusions from a story or article? Can you judge the author's purpose, mood, or tone?

DISCOVER THE MAIN IDEA

In certain kinds of reading materials—textbooks, encyclopedias, and "how-to" books, for example—a good writer helps you find the main thought quickly and easily. He uses signposts to help you. He may highlight the main thought by placing it in a center heading or in a side heading. He may feature this thought by putting it in *italics*.

Each paragraph should have a topic sentence that states the main thought. Near the end of the paragraph there may be a sentence that summarizes the paragraph. Some writers use such a summary as the topic sentence.

FIND THE SUPPORTING IDEAS

In a well-written paragraph, ideas are provided to support the main idea. These may be details that *explain* the main idea, or they may be additional information that *supports* or *proves* the main idea.

In the paragraphs that follow, notice the way in which the author presents her ideas:

Often, today, we hear arguments for and against the "development" of America's remaining areas of natural beauty. Among the developers are the officials of oil and lumber companies, who urge the exploitation of natural resources for private profit. Their case is strengthened by the fact that the benefits of business exploitation do reach the general public in some measure. A new lumber mill may provide hundreds of jobs in a depressed area, and oil deposits may send real estate values soaring.

Conservationists, on the other hand, argue that once land has been developed, it can never be "un-developed." Animals that are killed off are dead forever, and eventually an entire species may be wiped out. Often new jobs are only temporary; when a resource such as lumber is used up, the business moves away—and the jobless remain. Finally, the conservationists point out, exploiting a natural resource may injure another local industry, as, for example, when oil spills sweep over resort beaches, driving away thousands of tourists—and the money they might have spent.

The main and supporting ideas of these two paragraphs are outlined below:

1. Today many people argue that America's remaining wilderness areas should be open to business interests because:

    a) Business will benefit.

    b) Jobs will be provided.

    c) Land values may increase.

2. Conservationists oppose such unlimited expansion because:

    a) Spoiled areas of natural beauty often cannot be restored.

    b) Animal species may be wiped out.

    c) Economic gains may be temporary.

    d) Other resources may be harmed in the process of exploitation.

If you outline paragraphs in this way, you'll find it easier to determine the main idea and its supporting ideas.

CAN YOU FIND MAIN AND SUPPORTING IDEAS?

Read the next paragraph and find its main and supporting ideas. Write these ideas on the blank lines at the end of the paragraph.

Because the long western slope of the Sierra Nevada has a wide variety of temperatures and moisture conditions, this slope has clearly separated zones of natural vegetation. The first zone, in the foothills of the mountains up to an elevation of 1000 feet, is covered with grass and occasional oak trees. The second zone, between 1500 and 3000 feet, has scattered trees with yellow pine predominant. The third zone, between 3000 and 6000 feet, is heavily timbered. There the thick forests are watered by drenching rains. The fourth zone, above 6000 feet, has poor forest. Because of the cold temperatures and the thin soil of the rock surfaces, the trees are stunted.

Main idea: _____

Supporting ideas: _____

_____

_____

_____

_____

_____

_____

From your history or science textbook, select three paragraphs. Find and write down the main idea and the supporting ideas in each paragraph.

Why Do You Read?

A skilled reader reads for many specific purposes—for instance, to answer a particular question, to find a particular fact, or to form an opinion on a controversial issue. For each purpose, he uses specific reading skills. Some examples follow:

1. You may read to find the answer to a specific question, such as: What animals live in the arctic region? To find the answer, go to an encyclopedia. In the index look for the entry "Arctic." Find the number of the volume and the number of the page on which the article you're looking for appears.

When you've found the article, skim it—read a word, a phrase, or a sentence here and there on a page, but skip most of the words. While you skim, look for the names of arctic animals — for instance, caribou, foxes, wolves, polar bears. When you see any of these names, read the paragraph or paragraphs carefully and make notes on what you read.

You use the same types of reading skills in looking for a particular fact or for a statement to prove or disprove a point under discussion.

2. You may read to form an opinion on a topic such as a proposed state law on which there is much disagreement. Read carefully and thoughtfully the arguments in newspapers for and against the proposal. Then, on the basis of the evidence, make up your mind.

More Things to Do

Using a record like the one on page 28, keep a two-week record of your reading rates. Every day read two selections — one that is easy reading, such as a short story, and one that is more difficult, such as a textbook assignment. Record the results. After you've learned your reading rate for each type of material, set up a goal. Try to increase your reading rate to 350 words a minute for fiction and 250 words a minute for textbook material. At the end of the week you'll be able to see what gains you've made and how near you are to your goals.

Answers to exercises in this chapter:

Comprehension test: 1—0; 2—+; 3—0; 4—0; 5—+; 6—0; 7—+; 8—+; 9—0; 10—+

Vocabulary test: 1—abandon; 2—certify; 3—defy; 4—esteem; 5—ascertain

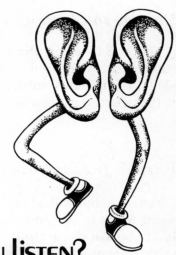

6·how well do you listen?

Listening is a very important way of learning—at home, at school, and elsewhere. At home you listen to your parents and learn from them—more often than you realize. At home you also hear radio and watch television programs—the news, dramas, movies.

You spend nearly half (45 percent) of your class time each day listening. You learn by listening to your teacher as he explains a textbook chapter or holds a question-and-answer period. You also learn by listening to other students during group discussion.

Learning to listen more effectively will help you become a better student. Pay close attention to what is said in class. Although you may do the talking occasionally, you will be listening most of the time. If you listen carefully and thoughtfully, you'll learn from what others say.

Students and teachers in one school made a survey of the kinds of situations students face daily. On the basis of this survey they prepared this list of listening activities:

1. Face-to-face conversations
2. Telephone conversations
3. Reports
4. Dramatizations
5. Assembly programs
6. Introductions
7. Discussions
8. Oral instructions
9. Announcements
10. Storytelling
11. Poetry
12. Choral speaking

In each of these activities, *the better you listen, the more you will learn.*

Compare Listening and Reading

Listening and reading are alike in many ways. When you hear a person make a speech or tell a story, and when you read the same speech or story, you get the same main ideas and the same supporting details. You get the same presentation of facts and opinions. You agree or disagree with the conclusions stated.

In other ways, however, listening and reading are very different. In listening you see the speaker, observe his changing facial expressions, and note the changes in his tone of voice. What you see and hear adds to your understanding of what is being said. In reading, you get the writer's ideas from the printed pages alone.

In listening to a speaker, you receive his ideas at the rate at which *he* chooses to present them. In reading, *you* determine this rate; you read as fast or as slowly as you please. In listening, you have to get an idea as it is presented. If you miss it at that point, it's "gone with the wind" as far as you're concerned. You must adapt your rate of absorbing ideas to the rate at which the speaker presents them. You must understand and analyze what he's saying while he's saying it. In reading, you can go back and reread either immediately or at a later time.

Listening, then, is a more demanding method of learning or study than reading is. Fortunately, however, even the fastest speaker presents ideas at a rate slower than the rate at which you would read them in print.

How Do You Listen?

You can listen in three main ways: purposefully, critically, and appreciatively. Certain skills, habits, and attitudes can help you learn to listen better in each of those ways.

Purposeful Listening

Your teacher talks because he has something worthwhile to say and a good reason for saying it. If you listen carefully, you may learn something you couldn't learn in any other way.

Furthermore, a teacher tries to make certain that a student who speaks has something valuable to say, a good reason for saying it, and someone to say it to. For these reasons it is important always to listen to the student who is speaking. That is not only a rule of courtesy—it is also a good way to learn.

You may engage in purposeful listening in many different situations—in a classroom, during dinner at home, and at a meeting of your club or community youth group.

To check your ability to listen, make a record of the listening you did yesterday. For each purpose given below, write one example:

1. To get an answer to your question

_____

2. To hear someone else's question

_____

3. To form an opinion on a topic

_____

4. To learn about a current news event

_____

5. To hear someone else's side of an argument

_____

6. To follow directions for doing something or going somewhere

_____

7. To obtain information on a topic of interest to you

_____

8. Other: _____

Critical Listening

Although critical listening is really another kind of purposeful listening, it is so important to good studying that we'll discuss it separately. In critical listening, you ask yourself such questions as these:

- Who is the speaker? Is he an expert on the subject of his talk?
- What is the speaker saying? Why is he saying it?
- Is the speaker presenting facts or opinions, or both? What are the sources of his facts? On what evidence are his opinions based?
- Do I agree or disagree with the speaker? Why?

To check your critical listening ability, listen carefully to a talk by a fellow student, an assembly speaker, or a prominent person on radio or TV. As you listen, make a brief record of what the speaker says, using this form:

MY RECORD OF A TALK
1. Name and occupation of the speaker
2. Title of his talk
3. The main idea presented
4. The supporting ideas presented
5. The speaker's general attitude toward his subject
6. A summary of the talk
7. My comments on the talk

Appreciative Listening

When you listen with appreciation, you search for values in both what the speaker is saying and in the way he is saying it. You may listen appreciatively to a lecture by a brilliant teacher, to an imaginative poem read by another student, or to a stirring movie or television program.

The appreciative listener is sensitive to the beauty or understanding displayed in a speech. The speaker may arouse your emotions and make you feel happy or unhappy, hopeful or fearful, angry or peaceful.

How Good Students Listen

When one group of students rated listening habits, they placed "quietness" and "appreciation" at the top of the list. Next, they listed the ability to think about what is being said. In addition, these students suggested the following standards for good listening:

1. Clear your desk except for a pencil and paper if you wish to take notes. Sit in a comfortable position with your eyes on the speaker. Don't fidget or make distracting noises.

2. Stay "with" the speaker. Don't let your mind wander.

3. Be patient if the speaker seems to be having difficulty with his speech or seems ill at ease.

4. Be ready and able to offer intelligent criticism of what the speaker has said or to ask thoughtful questions. Think of how you can use what you're hearing. Listen for mention of things to do and to read later.

5. If the final bell of a class period rings, don't interrupt the speaker. Give him time to say a few sentences that will conclude his talk.

6. Be courteous to the speaker and to other members of the audience. Don't whisper to your neighbor or write him notes. If you have to leave in the middle of the speech, get up and go as quickly as possible.

Are You a Good Listener?

If you're a good listener, you get the main ideas that are presented in a speech. You can tell the difference between a basic idea and a supporting fact. You can distinguish between the important and the unimportant.

No matter how good or how poor a listener you are, you can improve—by listening. Listen to and analyze your friends' remarks in class and ask them to analyze yours. In making your analysis, listen for the main ideas and the supporting ideas. Listen for opinions presented, as well.

As you listen to a classmate, be thoughtful and attentive even if his talk is rambling and poorly put together. If you have suggestions on how he might improve his talk, make them

friendly and constructive. Then ask him for his comments on your analysis of his talk. This will help you become a better listener.

Taking Notes Helps

As you improve your listening skills, you'll find you are able to listen to a speaker and take notes on his talk at the same time. Later, you may refer to those notes to recall specific information given in the talk.

A good notetaker never writes a complete sentence. He just jots down the *key* words and phrases he hears. Then, as soon as possible after the speech, he goes over his notes, filling in thoughts and ideas so that the notes will still be meaningful to him days or weeks later. Here is an example of a brief talk; notes taken during the talk; and the same notes after the notetaker has checked them over:

Speech: "George Washington is often called the 'father of his country.' During the Revolutionary War he commanded the American troops, turning a collection of farmers, shopkeepers, and rough frontiersmen into an effective fighting force. Later, as every American student knows, he became the first president of the United States."

Notes: _____

Notes after checking: _____

What Are the Important Listening Skills?

A good listener can—

1. *Recall ideas.* You should be able to remember the principal ideas of a speech and be able to answer questions about the speech.

2. *Follow directions.* A good listener can remember and follow oral instructions.

3. *Recognize essential ideas.* You should be able to identify and classify ideas according to their importance—to follow the speaker's organization of ideas and understand his summary statements.

4. *Understand the meanings of words.* You should be able to understand the meanings of many unfamiliar words in context. For example, the sentence *The savory smells from the kitchen made him realize how hungry he was* gives you a broad hint — which the good listener should be able to pick up — as to the meaning of the word *savory.*

5. *Comprehend ideas.* This skill enables you to get at the main points of a speech and draw your own conclusions from them.

Are You a Good Listener?

Rate yourself as a listener. Read each of the questions that follow. Then make a check in the appropriate column (Always, Sometimes, or Rarely) at the right of the question.

	Always	Some-times	Rarely
1. Do you get ready for listening?	_____	_____	_____
2. Do you pay close attention to what you hear?	_____	_____	_____
3. Do you show courtesy toward the speaker and the rest of the audience?	_____	_____	_____
4. Do you recognize the main ideas of a speech?	_____	_____	_____
5. (After you've worked at improving your listening skills, try taking notes during a speech.) Do your notetaking skills improve with practice?	_____	_____	_____
6. Do you listen for significant details?	_____	_____	_____
7. Do you feel the emotions the speaker tries to get across			

	Always	Some-times	Rarely
and see and hear, in your mind, the sights and sounds he describes?	_____	_____	_____
8. Do you get the correct meaning of new words from the context of a speech?	_____	_____	_____
9. Do you take accurate notes on a speech?	_____	_____	_____
10. Do you write a short summary of the important ideas in a speech?	_____	_____	_____

To become a better listener, work to improve the skills and habits you just checked under "sometimes" or "rarely."

The better you listen, the more you'll learn, understand, and remember. Therefore, begin now to help yourself listen more skillfully. Because you can learn so much by using your ears, listening is very important.

More Things to Do

1. Select one of the subjects you're studying — English, for example. Then estimate the percentage of your English time (classwork and studying) you spend on each of the following means of communication: listening, reading, speaking, writing.

2. Is it easier for you, by listening or by reading —

　　a) to recognize main ideas and supporting ideas?
　　b) to follow the organization of a topic?
　　c) to draw your own conclusions about a topic?

3. Make a checklist of things you can do to improve your listening. Check the list every day for two weeks. At the end of that time see if you can notice any improvement in your listening habits. Which of the things you did helped you improve? Which of the items on your list need more practice?

7 • WRITE it RIGHT!

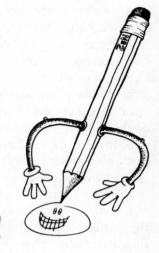

You may not plan to write a great novel or become a newsmagazine reporter. You should, however, be able to write competently—for your studies and in your personal life as well. You probably will have to know how to write a good business letter or an interesting friendly letter. Frequently you have to write reports, themes, compositions, and other papers for your school-work. Writing *is* an essential study skill. A large part of your school success depends on your ability to express yourself clearly on paper.

There's no great mystery about how to improve your writing skills. Just write. And then write some more. When novelist Sinclair Lewis was asked how he learned to write, he answered, "By wearing out the seat of my pants on a chair."

If you wish to become a more effective writer, make this one of your chief goals in the days ahead. Learn and practice good writing, using the techniques this chapter suggests.

What Makes Good Writing?

Here are tips to help you improve your writing:

1. *Know what you want to write about.* The ideas may be your own or someone else's. If you borrow another's ideas, however, be sure to give credit for them.

2. *Develop and follow a well-organized outline.*

3. *Express yourself*—your personality, feelings, opinions, imagination, and originality.

4. *Use the style that is most appropriate* to what you're writing. If you're writing a factual report, use explanation and examples. If it's a short story, use descriptions and conversation. If it's a poem, use rhythm and meter.

5. *Use simple, vivid words*—words that help the reader see, hear, smell, and feel what you're describing—words such as *murmur, dismal, crackle, slime, rustle, forlorn, plunge, lazy, whisper.*

6. *Try to use the best words for your purpose.*

7. *Check and recheck your grammar, spelling, and punctuation.*

Adapt your writing to your purpose. *What* are you writing? *Why* are you writing it? What do you hope to *accomplish*? *Who* will read it?

For example, you might write an editorial for your school newspaper urging students to support the school's antilitter campaign. Address this editorial directly to the students. Use short sentences and short paragraphs to make the editorial sharp and fast-reading. Include humor to amuse your readers and hold their attention.

Getting Ready to Write

Whatever kind of writing you undertake—reporting for a school paper, composing an essay, writing a business letter—follow these steps:

1. *Decide what to write about.* If you're writing a composition on a topic of your own choice, select a subject that interests you or that you

already know something about. If it interests you, you're more likely to enjoy writing about it. Knowing something about the topic gives you a head start because you already have some of the information you need.

2. *Prepare an outline.* Decide what *aspect* of your subject you'll write about. Once you've decided, you can determine what information you'll need. As you gather information you may get new ideas about the topic. If this happens, revise your outline.

3. *Gather information.* You can collect information about your topic in a number of ways. For instance, *observe* yourself, other people, things, events. Make notes on what you see, hear, and feel. *Interview* someone—a local person who is well informed on your topic. This person may be a relative, a businessman, a labor leader, a postman, or perhaps the district attorney. *Read* about your topic in books, magazines, newspapers.

How to Get Information

Observation. Suppose you're writing about something you've experienced—a summer job as a camp counselor, for example. For information, you'll rely mainly on what *you* observed and remember. If you made notes at the time of the experience, they'll be a big help.

Whether or not you made on-the-spot notes, write down first all the facts and impressions you can recall. To refresh your memory, you may want to talk with someone who shared the experience with you.

For practice, select as a topic for a composition any personal experience—a trip, a party, a sports event, or a person you met. On the lines that follow, write down your observations about this experience.

_____

_____

_____

_____

_____

Interviews. A newspaper reporter often interviews people to get facts for a story. For example, if he is writing about a big fire, he talks with the fire chief whose men put out the blaze. He talks with the owner of the building that burned. He talks with the people who got out of the building in time. Through such interviews he gets the facts, figures, opinions, and colorful, interesting details he needs to write his story.

Like a reporter, you can use interviews to collect information for what you plan to write. Suppose you're writing about your school's football season. To get ideas, you talk to the coach of the team, to the players, to the cheerleaders, to the high school principal, and to local businessmen. You'll use the information you gather to write your story.

Before you interview anyone for information, think about and write down questions you want to ask. During the interview take notes on what the person says.

Suppose you're writing a report on a career you hope to have. Suppose also that you expect to interview a person who has been very successful in a similar career. Before the interview think about and write here the questions you would want to ask this person:

1. _____

2. _____

3. _____

4. _____

Reading. For most topics you will write about, you can gather ideas through reading. You can do this reading in the classroom, in the school library, in the public library, and at home. You can refer to textbooks, encyclopedias, yearbooks, and other reference books. (Suggestions on how to use the library and the important reference materials in it appear in chapter 10.)

While reading to get ideas, facts, and figures for your composition, make notes on useful items. If you record these notes on cards, you can easily arrange the cards in the proper order.

Sit Down and—Write

Before you started your composition, you wrote a research outline that showed you what information you had and what you needed. As ideas came to you, you revised the outline. As you observed, interviewed, and read, you made notes on useful information. Those notes are your *source materials*. Now you'll use both your outline and your notes as you take the next steps in writing:

1. *Organize your notes.* Have them in front of you. Read and organize them. If the notes are on cards, you can readily sort them into groups according to the major and minor headings in your outline. If the notes are on sheets of paper, organize them according to headings on new sheets of paper. (As you can see, it's more convenient to have the notes on cards.) Whichever method you use, you may at this time discard some notes and add others.

In organizing your notes you may revise the ideas that appear in your outline. You may also change the supporting ideas for each main idea.

Sometimes, as you rearrange your notes, you see more clearly the main ideas that bear on the topic.

2. *Prepare your writing outline.* After organizing and revising your outline and notes, draw up your writing outline. This outline will cover all the principal and supporting ideas you wish to write about.

Why bother to make an outline? The answer is that if you develop a good outline before starting to write, your composition will be clearer and better organized. You'll also save yourself time and energy because you won't have to keep rewriting unsuccessful, poorly organized drafts.

For practice in preparing an outline for a report, organize the following notes that deal with teen-agers' contributions to society. You are given two lists—list A and list B. You are to match the two lists. *First,* read all the notes in list A. Each note is a statement. *Second,* write the key number of each *useful* note on the line of list B where it belongs. When you've finished, you'll find there are five statements left over in list A that have no place in this outline.

List A

Notes on "How Do Teen-agers Contribute to Society?"

1. Most teen-agers have brothers and sisters.

2. Teen-agers can take part in neighborhood cleanups.

3. You become a voter at age eighteen.

4. If you study hard, you'll make lots of money.

5. Teen-agers can offer a good example to younger brothers and sisters.

6. Church groups, scouts, and other organizations often call for volunteers to help organize activities for the younger children.

7. Teen-agers have been at the forefront of movements to assure equal rights for all Americans.

8. You get out of life only as much as you give.

9. Students should be careful of school property.

10. Parents can expect family cooperation from teen-agers.

11. Many students prepare for future responsibilities by holding class offices.

12. Teen-agers who can travel have a chance to learn about their country.

13. Teen-agers should be required to do chores to earn their allowances.

14. Voter-registration drives are often manned by teen-agers.

15. Every year, fewer teen-agers drop out of school.

16. Teen-agers and their parents can try to develop mutual respect, if not total agreement, on all issues.

17. Hospitals usually need volunteer workers.

18. Students could help organize a public recreation facility.

19. Good students are a credit to their school.

20. Teen-agers may serve in the Peace Corps.

List B

Writing outline for "How Do Teen-agers Contribute to Society?"

I. Contributions to home and family life
   A. _____
   B. _____
   C. _____
   D. _____

II. Contributions to school
   A. _____
   B. _____
   C. _____

III. Contributions to the community
   A. _____
   B. _____
   C. _____
   D. _____

IV. Contributions to national affairs
   A. _____
   B. _____
   C. _____
   D. _____

(Answers are at the end of the chapter.)

In this exercise you were given the main headings for a written report—a real help in organizing the notes. Ordinarily, you yourself would have to supply the main headings.

3. *Revise your outline again if necessary.* Your writing outline is like the blueprint for building a house. Before construction starts, you may make major changes in the blueprint. After it starts, you may make minor changes in details.

As you write, you may revise your outline. Although you may make some changes in it as you rewrite, the outline gives direction and organization to your writing. In other words, you should think of your outline as a guide to what you're writing—not as a straitjacket that keeps you from writing freely and naturally.

Other Kinds of Writing

Writing a report, composition, or theme based on facts, figures, and ideas you have observed or collected is just *one* kind of writing. Let's look at two other kinds of writing required in school—the short story and the book report.

Short-Story Writing

The short story is one of the most popular forms of modern literature—and a good area for writing practice, too. A short story may be *factual*—based on a true experience, your own or another's. It may be fictional—based on an imaginary event. It may combine fact *and* fiction.

Whether your short story is true or fictional, remember that it usually has this main characteristic—*it presents one single important idea.*

Short-Story Ideas

You can find ideas for short stories by—

1. *Thinking about your own experiences.* You may select an experience that was unusual or dramatic. Then you may write about this experience and the mood you felt at the time—joy, sadness, or whatever.

You may write this story in the first person (I did...I felt...) or in the third person (he did...he felt...). If you write in the third person, you tell the story through the actions, thoughts, and words of other characters—not your own.

2. *Listening to other people.* You may pick up story ideas just by keeping your ears open. For instance, if your grandparents tell you about the "good old days," you might use this information in story writing.

3. *Observing people, places, and things.* Looking and listening at home, at school, and in the community give you many story ideas. If you're a good observer, you note and write down interesting points about a person, place, thing, or event.

4. *Reading—reading—reading!* By wide reading of books, magazines, and newspapers, you may come across an idea for a short story. Good feature items often can be found buried in the back pages of a newspaper.

5. *Using your imagination.* Suppose you see a boy fishing from a high dock. Let your imagination go. What if he hooks an unusually large

fish? Or imagine that he hooks something other than a fish. What might it be? How did it get there? Or suppose you see a fully dressed man lying on the beach. Who is he? Why is he there? Is he dead or alive?

6. *Choosing a theme and developing it.* Your theme might be "Who travels fastest travels alone" or "You must be a friend to have a friend." You can develop a short story to illustrate and comment on such themes.

7. *Asking why.* Why do people act in various ways—bravely, imaginatively, foolishly? Select a situation—a young person volunteering for the Peace Corps, for example, and tell why he did so. To travel? To get away from home? To contribute to society?

Writing Book Reports

In preparing a book report, keep your readers —teacher or classmates—in mind. If you like a book very much and write a glowing report on it, your report may inspire others to read the same book.

In preparing a book report, you might follow these tips:

1. Ask and answer such questions as these: Is the story good? Why? Who are the main characters? Does the book give a clear picture of the period or place with which it deals? Is it worth reading? Why, or why not?

2. Do *not* write page after page retelling the story in detail or giving away its ending. Either will bore your reader—besides spoiling the book for him.

3. In your own words write a little about each of the most interesting parts of the book.

4. If you liked or disliked parts of the book, say so—and tell why. If you were enthusiastic about the book, let yourself go—write what you think and feel.

5. If the book was informative nonfiction, write briefly what you learned from it.

6. Try to make the report as interesting as possible. Avoid a dull listing of facts.

7. In a report on either fiction or nonfiction, include your evaluation of the book. Tell what you think the author tried to do and whether you believe he succeeded.

What Is Good Writing?

Whatever you're writing, consider what professional writers do to produce good writing— writing that people readily understand and enjoy.

To see the features of good writing, read articles that appear in popular magazines carried by the public library. Read each article as you usually would—for information or enjoyment. Then reread it to study the opening paragraph and how the author puts words together to say what he wants to say. Studying what a good professional writer has written can teach you a great deal about how to write clearly and interestingly. Following are some writing tips to keep in mind:

1. *Self-expression.* In your writing be your real self. Reveal something of your personality— of your thoughts and feelings about matters. Put some "you" into the words you write.

Avoid stale expressions such as "out on a limb," "had his ears pinned back," and "sly as a fox." Such expressions are called "bromides" —they put the reader to sleep.

Instead, try to think of fresh ways of saying things. That is what Carl Sandburg did when he wrote "The fog comes on little cat feet." And that is what Rupert Brooke did when he wrote of "the rough male kiss of blankets." Each of these writers used words that create pictures in the reader's mind.

2. *Attention-winning leads.* Catch the reader's interest in your *first* paragraph. Never put him off with "I am going to write about..." Instead, make the reader want to read more— but don't tell him now how the story comes out.

As a lead for a story, which do you think is better—paragraph A or paragraph B?

A. If you have a vacation this summer, you may wish to visit one of the great public parks in the United States. You may choose Yellowstone National Park as your destination. This park charges only a small admission fee.

B. Vacation time! Where are you going on your trip? Are you camping out? If so, you might visit one of our national parks. These public playgrounds offer all forms of outdoor enjoyment and charge only a small admission price.

While there is nothing actually wrong with paragraph A, paragraph B starts out in a much more lively fashion. It captures your interest immediately by sounding a note of excitement that most of us associate with vacation time.

Both paragraphs illustrate a way of opening a nonfiction article. Each gives a little information about the subject to be covered in the rest of the article.

3. *Conversation.* Employ conversation to give a story life. For example, consider this story about a rainy afternoon:

"I sure wish this rain would let up. This makes two games in a row that have been called off." Jim turned from the window scowling.

"Well, it can't rain forever." Mrs. Gordon secretly thought it might, but she wasn't going to say so. "Instead of wasting the afternoon grumping about the weather, why not take advantage of it? I have a fine idea..."

Jim looked up expectantly.

4. *Examples for illustration.* By giving an example from time to time, you make your points clearer. You also increase the interest of the article. The following anecdote might be part of a story about people who insist on telling *all* they know about a subject.

While a father and his small son were visiting the zoo, they came to the pool where the penguins lived. The son seemed so interested in these strange birds that his father obtained a 600-page scientific book on penguins. He gave this book to his son.

The boy worked hard at the book. Finally, after about two months, he finished it and handed it to his father.

His father said, "Well, how did you like the book?"

The son replied, "Oh, I guess it was all right. But it told me more about penguins than I wanted to know!"

5. *Effective concluding paragraphs.* An excellent—and enjoyable—way to learn how to write effective concluding paragraphs is to read some of the short stories of O. Henry. Like many good short-story writers, he uses the final paragraph for a surprise ending, or "twist."

In nonfiction, too, strong final paragraphs are important. If you're writing a historical account, you'll end it with a summary paragraph. For instance, you may be writing a report on the first people who inhabited North America as revealed by the study of Indian relics in Arizona. You may sum up your report by a statement such as this: "All the evidence indicates that people from Asia migrated across the Bering Strait thousands of years ago. They discovered America."

In writing the last paragraph or sentence, avoid stating the dull or the obvious. For instance, in a letter, don't say: "Having nothing more to write, I will end this letter."

The final paragraph of your composition in a sense serves as a cord that ties the earlier parts together in a neat package.

6. *Logical, well-organized paragraphs.* Each paragraph should have an interesting lead, or topic sentence. The other sentences explain or illustrate the topic sentence.

Always try to write a sentence that flows naturally from the sentence before it and into the next one. If the sentences in a paragraph jump from one idea to a completely unrelated idea, you'll mystify the reader.

Whenever possible, make paragraphs fairly short. For easier reading and for better understanding, write many short paragraphs instead of a few long ones.

7. *Short sentences.* A long sentence (more than twenty-five words in length) is usually harder to follow than a short sentence. As examples, consider the following two paragraphs. Read both and tell which is easier to understand.

A. Although the lesson has progressed favorably, the teacher was having difficulty with his explanation because the class was distracted by a private conference two pupils were having in the back of the room.

B. Although the lesson had progressed favorably, the teacher had difficulty with his explanation. The class was distracted by a private conference of two pupils in the back of the room.

In general, try to write short sentences. If you've written a long sentence, try to break it up into two or three short ones. To do so, it may be necessary to shift the order of the wording or the ideas. Omit all superfluous words. For practice, rewrite this long sentence by breaking it into four short sentences:

Since I plan to enter my father's business after I graduate from high school, I am studying commercial courses, but I do know the value of a college program to a person who wants to succeed in life, and I wonder sometimes whether it would be better for me to change my plans.

_____

_____

_____

_____

Use the Right Words

As you write a fictional story or a nonfiction article, select the words that will best get across what you wish to say. Try to use the right word in the right place. Remember the following rules:

1. *Use familiar, everyday language.* The best writers use many common, everyday words. They may also employ colorful words. They may use a word that the context defines—for example: "For him, nothing but the most delicate sauces, the subtlest herbs, the finest fruits— he was indeed an *epicure*."

Taking a tip from good writers, employ everyday words, but throw in some that challenge the reader's thinking or his imagination.

In writing technical articles, you may have to use some unfamiliar technical words. In a composition titled "The Hydrogen Bomb and World Peace," you will probably have to use words such as *strategic, parliamentary, isolationism.*

2. *Use exact words.* The English language is one of the richest languages in the world. From it you can choose words that have many different shades of meaning. You can use these words to tell the reader exactly what you mean.

3. *Use vivid words.* You can improve your writing by using vivid words—words that have

life in them. For example, in writing about autumn leaves, tell about their shades of scarlet, purple, yellow, and brown; about their rustling, crackling sounds; about their dry, crisp, harsh feel; about their dusty, pungent smell.

Main Steps in Writing

To summarize what you've studied in this chapter, consider the main writing steps:

1. *Write the first draft.* In this draft follow your writing outline. Put down the whole story, from beginning to end. In the first draft your principal goal is to get the entire story on paper— to write quickly all the ideas you want to include.

2. *Revise.* After you've written the first draft, read it carefully and *critically.* Will your opening paragraph capture the reader's attention? If not, try to improve it. Then examine each of the other paragraphs in turn to see whether they develop the story or article idea by idea. Last, read the final paragraph to determine whether it is a good closing, one with "punch."

Next, check on the sentences that make up each paragraph. Ask yourself: Does the paragraph have a topic sentence? Do the other sentences explain the leading sentence? Does each sentence flow from the one just before it?

Here is an example of a paragraph written and edited by a high school student:

Late in the afternoon we saw a small ~~iland~~ *island* up ahead and decided to camp ~~there~~ *there* for the night. ~~because~~ *We knew* ~~we know~~ if we waited much ~~later~~ *longer* it would be ~~so~~ *too* dark to find a camping place. ~~It~~ Dad ~~steered~~ *steered* the canoe into a low ~~place in the~~ *place on* shore, and I jumped out and pulled ~~it up~~ *the boat* onto the grass. ~~and~~ Dad jumped out ~~to.~~ *too.* ~~Their~~ *There* was a big tree near where we had landed, and we decided that would be a good spot for a camp. ~~But as~~ *As* we found out ~~latter~~ *later* we couldn't ~~of~~ *have* picked a ~~worst~~ *worse* spot.

(Notice that the writer, in editing his paragraph, added a better lead sentence, broke up an overlong following sentence, corrected spelling, and improved on his wording.)

3. *Check grammar, punctuation, and spelling.* In any story or article, you try to communicate with the reader. Be as clear and as accurate as possible. Check carefully on three writing-related skills—grammar (English usage), punctuation, and spelling.

For practice in writing, do the following exercises. The correct answers are at the end of this chapter.

Grammar. Read each of the following sentences. If a sentence is grammatically correct, write *R* at the left of it. If there is an error in the sentence, write *W* beside it. Then cross out the error in each sentence you marked *W* and write in the correction.

_____ 1. Civics is my favorite subject.

_____ 2. Each have taken his place.

_____ 3. The coach called he and I.

_____ 4. This bike is Jack and Joe's.

_____ 5. I will be late tonight.

_____ 6. No one has laid any coats here.

_____ 7. The teacher likes you as well as me.

_____ 8. He has drove home.

_____ 9. You was absent yesterday.

_____10. Where is the teen-age dance at?

Punctuation. To check on your ability to punctuate correctly, read each sentence and then put in the correct punctuation marks.

1. Rochester New York is a manufacturing center for mens clothing
2. The West was not yet opened and no one knew what opportunities it offered
3. Ships are painted and repaired drydocks are used for this purpose
4. Why did you go away
5. Johns mother asked did you lose your hat

Spelling. To check on your ability to spell, examine the two words in item 1. Decide which spelling is correct—A or B. Write the letter of the correct spelling at the left of number 1. Do each of the other items in the same way.

_____1. (A) separate   (B) seperate

_____2. (A) truely   (B) truly

_____3. (A) absense   (B) absence

_____4. (A) recommend   (B) reccomend

_____5. (A) independent   (B) independant

Because you may find it difficult to check on English usage, punctuation, and spelling all at the same time, you may wish to read and correct your composition three times. *First,* check for grammar, or English usage. *Second,* check for punctuation. *Third,* check for spelling.

Summary

For any kind of good writing, you need ideas. You must also know how and where to find them. You may obtain ideas by observing, interviewing, reading, and using your imagination.

As you gather ideas for writing, write them down as notes. Prepare an outline and organize your notes according to it. Referring to this filled-in outline, try to express your ideas in a direct and simple style. Try to write an interesting opening paragraph and an effective closing paragraph. Use familiar words and short sentences.

Write and then revise, again and again, until you have a good composition. Next, check over your composition to find and correct errors in English usage, punctuation, and spelling.

More Things to Do

1. For several days keep a written record of materials you can use in writing a composition. Write an outline for your composition. Write the first draft. Then revise and correct it.

2. From daily or Sunday newspapers and from magazines, clip several examples of each of the following kinds of writing: (*a*) an article or es-

say; (b) a news story; (c) a short story; (d) a book review. Study the writing used in each example.

3. Stretch your imagination. What words can you think of to complete each of the following?

a) bright as _____

b) lovely as _____

c) rough as _____

d) quiet as _____

e) loud as _____

f) swift as _____

● **Answers** to exercises in this chapter:

Outline for "How Do Teen-agers Contribute to Society?": I—5, 10, 13, 16; II—9, 11, 19; III—2, 6, 17, 18; IV—3, 7, 14, 20

English Usage
R 1. Civics is my favorite subject.
           has
W 2. Each have taken his place.
                   him   me
W 3. The coach called he and I.

R 4. This bike is Jack and Joe's.
R 5. I will be late tonight.
R 6. No one has laid any coats here.
R 7. The teacher likes you as well as me.
           driven
W 8. He has drove home.
           were
W 9. You was absent yesterday.
W 10. Where is the teen-age dance at?
       (Or even better: Where is the teen-age dance being held?)

Punctuation
1. Rochester, New York, is a manufacturing center of men's clothing.
2. The West was not yet opened, and no one knew what opportunities it offered.
3. Ships are painted and repaired; drydocks are used for this purpose.
4. Why did you go away?
5. John's mother asked, "Did you lose your hat?"

Spelling
1. A. separate
2. B. truly
3. B. absence
4. A. recommend
5. A. independent

8·how do you read—without words?

Oooops! What's going on here? What is about to happen? What might have happened a few seconds earlier? How do you think the man feels? What might he be saying?

You can answer these questions at once— almost without thinking. This drawing tells a simple "story," and you can "read" it quickly. This picture is worth a thousand words—just as the old proverb says.

As you study, you will come across pictures— and other visual materials—that are worth many thousands of words. Such materials include maps, charts, graphs, and cartoons. Of course, most visuals in textbooks, encyclopedias, and other study sources are more complex than the drawing above. They can, however, be far clearer and easier to understand than the written-out information would be. They can show you at a glance facts that would need pages and pages of words in explanation. If you learn to read and interpret visuals quickly and accurately, you'll save many hours of study time. This chapter will help you learn how.

Reading Maps

A person in a jet plane flying several miles above the earth can see great bodies of land and sea spread out below. As he scans the landscape he looks for clues to tell him exactly what he's seeing. He knows that deep blue marks oceans, lakes, and rivers. Deserts appear tannish gray. Irregular blue shapes cutting into land areas are bays and harbors. Brown fingers that stretch into the ocean are capes and peninsulas. At night large cities are a sparkle of white lights and neon signs.

Like a flyer you can see great areas of the earth at a glance—on maps. The maps you use in studying have clues to help you understand them. Some of the most common are listed below. Nearly all maps have some—or all—of these clues.

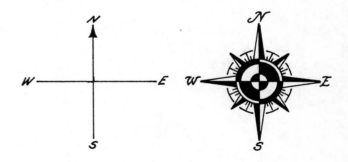

• *Directional indicator.* Usually, north is toward the top of the map, south toward the bottom, east toward the right, and west toward the left.

However, this is not always so. For example, a mapmaker might draw a map of a city showing the city's major streets running straight up and down and across. But suppose the major streets actually run northeast to southwest, not directly north to south. Then the mapmaker will have to "tilt" the map. The directional indicator will show that north is toward the top *left* edge of the map.

SCALE OF MILES 0 —— 5 —— 10 —— 15 —— 20
One inch equals about 10.8 miles

• *Scale of miles.* Maps are of many different sizes, and the size of the areas they show may vary greatly as well. (Compare the areas shown on the maps on these pages, for example.) To help you figure out the size of the area shown on any given map, a scale of miles is included. It tells how many miles of countryside are represented by each inch on the map. Using the scale, you can measure the straight-line distance between any two points on the map.

• *Latitude and longitude.* Latitude and longitude are two sets of imaginary lines that are often drawn on maps. (See page 51.) They can help you locate accurately any spot on earth.

The lines of latitude, or *parallels,* run east-west and are measured in degrees. The equator is at 0° latitude. The first parallel to the north is 10° north latitude; the first to the south is 10° south latitude. The North Pole is at 90°N. What do you think is the latitude of the South Pole? _____

The north-south lines, or *meridians,* are the lines of longitude. They measure distances east and west of an imaginary line that runs through England. This line, called the *prime meridian,* is at 0° longitude. East of this line is east longitude. It extends halfway round the world. West of the prime meridian is west longitude. It meets east longitude in the Pacific Ocean. In all, there are 360 degrees of longitude, 180 east and 180 west.

• *Map symbols.* On every good map the map symbols are explained in a key, usually at the bottom of the map. These symbols are the

"language" in which the map is written, and you must understand them in order to read the map. Many map symbols are standardized. That is, they are used by all mapmakers. One example of a standardized symbol is the shield that represents a U.S. numbered highway. Others are the lines that show different degrees of longitude and latitude. Dots or circles stand for cities, thin lines for rivers, dotted lines for boundaries.

• *Special legends.* Many maps are designed to show more than simple geography; thus they may use special symbols that are not standardized. For example, a population map may use different colors to indicate various population densities. Another map may show the goods produced in an area. The map key shows the symbols used—for example, an ear of corn to represent corn-growing regions or a fish to indicate the fishing industry. (See map above.)

These are some of the clues that will help you read maps quickly and easily. Use them as you study each of the following maps, and answer the questions about each one.

Study the map on page 51. You may want to check an atlas to help you answer the following questions:

1. What area is shown? _____ Which way is north? _____ Locate and label: Atlantic Ocean, Pacific Ocean, Gulf of Mexico, Great Lakes, Canada, Mexico.

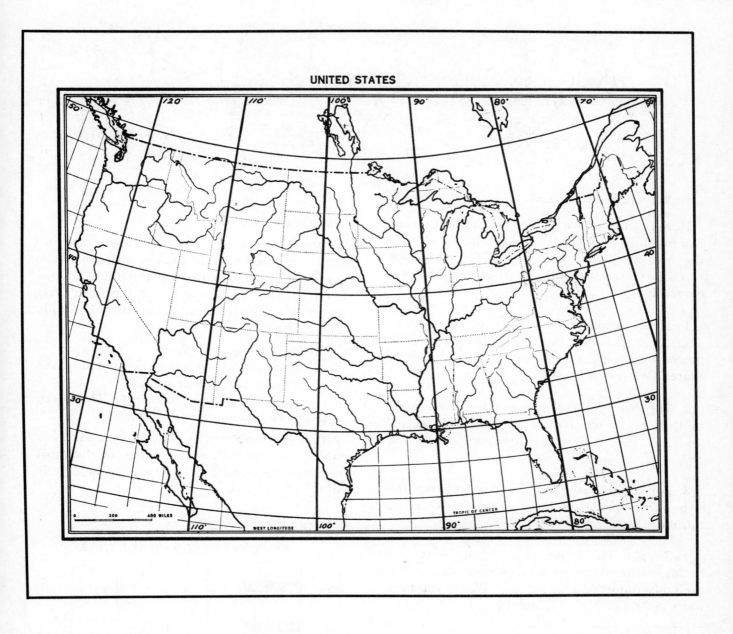

2. How many miles are shown to the inch? _____ About how long is our west coast? _____

3. Locate and label the following cities, using an atlas if necessary: New York; Washington; Miami; New Orleans; Dallas; Denver; Chicago; San Francisco. Will you use the same symbol for all of them?

4. Which major river systems are shown? _____ In which general direction does each flow? _____ What mountain ranges are shown? _____

5. Note the lines of latitude and longitude. At their farthest extents, to what degrees of latitude and longitude do the 48 contiguous states of the United States reach? _____

6. The latitude and longitude of Philadelphia, Pennsylvania, are approximately 40°N, 75°W. Can you find the city without referring to another map?

7. By looking at lines of latitude and longitude you can estimate the true direction of one place from another. Find Philadelphia on the map. What city that you have already labeled on your map of the United States is directly west of it? _____

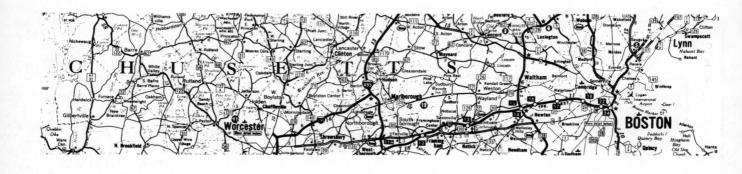

Scale of Miles

Lambert Conformal Projection   ONE INCH EQUALS ABOUT 10.9 MILES   1:690,000

Here is a map for which close, thorough study is a must. Read it wrong and you may end up in the Atlantic Ocean! To answer the questions, you'll have to look at the map and its key very carefully.

1. This map shows a section of the state of _____. Can you locate this area on the preceding map? on the map of the United States? Why, or why not?

2. Suppose you want to travel from Worcester to Boston. In what direction will you travel? _____ About how many miles will you go? _____

3. For the fastest possible drive between the two cities, you would probably choose route number _____. Why?

4. Suppose you want to travel from Worcester to Marlboro. What route numbers would you probably follow? _____ Would you take route 290? _____ Explain. _____
_____

5. List the following cities and towns in order of size, from smallest to largest. How does the map help you do this?

Marlboro _____
Woodville _____
Boston _____
Hopkinton _____
Watertown _____
_____
_____
_____

6. What does the map suggest about population distribution in this area? _____
_____
_____

Reading Graphs

Graphs are used to present figures on a subject for a given time or over a period of time. Because a graph's figures are given in a simple, visual pattern, it is easy to compare the facts and to remember them later. As you read a graph, it is important to—

- *Read the title of the graph.*
- *Read the scale for the graph.* This scale gives relative amounts or percentages.
- *Look for the source of the graph.* This often appears as a footnote near the graph.

Although there are many different kinds of graphs, we will look at only three of the most common: a bar graph, a line graph, and a circle graph.

BAR GRAPH

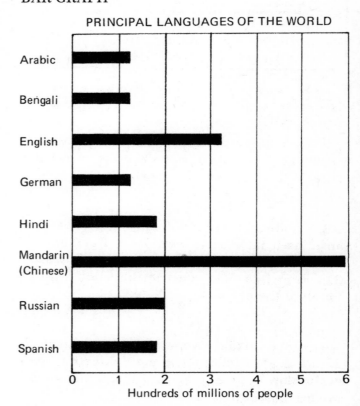

PRINCIPAL LANGUAGES OF THE WORLD

Arabic

Bengali

English

German

Hindi

Mandarin (Chinese)

Russian

Spanish

0   1   2   3   4   5   6

Hundreds of millions of people

The bar graph is useful for presenting and comparing figures on a particular subject for a given year. For example, figure 4 shows the approximate number of people who spoke each of the world's most common languages in 1971.

1. Which part of this graph describes its purpose? _____

2. In reading a graph look first at the labels along its vertical and horizontal axes. The vertical axis is the up-and-down line farthest to the left. What are its labels? _____ How are they arranged? _____ The horizontal axis is the line along the bottom. What do the numbers 0–600 stand for? _____ What clue tells you the numbers they represent?
_____

3. In 1971, what was the world's principal language? _____

4. In 1971, about how many people spoke Hindi? _____ How many spoke English? _____ Spanish? _____

5. From this graph you can infer that in 1971 the world's most heavily populated country was _____.

Another common type of graph is the picture graph. If this bar graph were redrawn as a picture graph, the numbers along the horizontal axis would not be needed. Instead, a symbol would represent a certain number of people. Suppose the symbol stood for 500,000 people. Then, after the label "Russian," there would be four symbols, representing a total of two million people. As an exercise, make up a symbol and draw this graph as a picture graph.

LINE GRAPHS

Line graphs are used to show trends over a period of years. Figure 5 shows how immigration from two foreign countries into the United States changed between 1950 and 1970. The vertical axis shows, in thousands, the number of immigrants. The horizontal axis shows each year from 1950 to 1970, although only each five-year period is labeled.

Suppose you want to know the figure for immigration from Canada in 1960. Find the year 1960 at the bottom of the graph. Move your eyes upward along the vertical guide line until they reach the dotted line that stands for Canada. Next, from the dotted line move your eyes horizontally to the left until they reach the vertical axis. There they focus on the number 30. So you know that in 1960, 30,000 Canadian immigrants entered the United States.

HOW U.S. IMMIGRATION HAS CHANGED

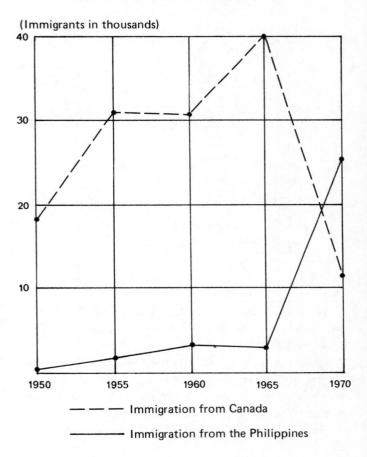

------- Immigration from Canada

——— Immigration from the Philippines

1. Unlike the bar graph, the line graph has a key. Why is it necessary? _____

2. In 1950 immigration from Canada was about _____. From the Philippines, it was about _____.

3. In what year did immigration from the Philippines first exceed 10,000? _____

4. Over what five-year spans did immigration from Canada drop? _____ By about how much in each case? _____

HOW OUR JOBS HAVE CHANGED

Per cent of labor force in various occupations

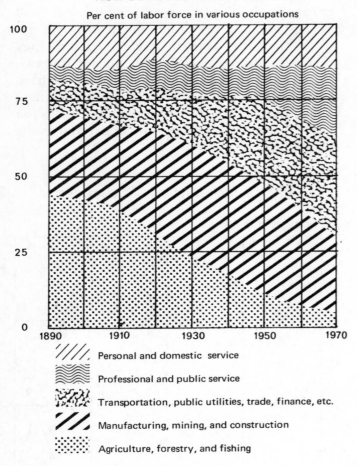

Personal and domestic service

Professional and public service

Transportation, public utilities, trade, finance, etc.

Manufacturing, mining, and construction

Agriculture, forestry, and fishing

3. In which two groups of occupations did the percentages of the working people increase the most between 1890 and 1970?_____
_____

4. According to this graph, have job opportunities increased (a) in agriculture?_____; (b) in professional and public service?_____.

CIRCLE GRAPH

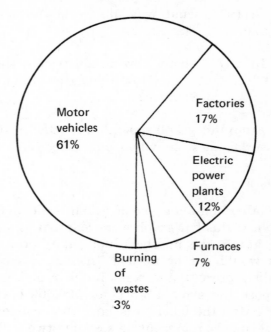

Major Sources of Air Pollution

Motor vehicles 61%

Factories 17%

Electric power plants 12%

Furnaces 7%

Burning of wastes 3%

Above is a more complex line graph. It shows the percentages for each census year, 1890 through 1970, of workers who were employed in various occupational groups—in personal and domestic service, for instance. From this graph you will find it somewhat difficult to estimate for a given census year the exact percentage for each occupational group. Even so, you will find the graph helpful in answering such key questions as these:

1. About what percentage of America's working people were in jobs in agriculture, forestry, and fishing in 1890? _____ percent. In 1970? _____ percent.

2. Between 1890 and 1970, what happened to the percentage of working people who had jobs in manufacturing, mining, and construction?

_____

_____

One of the best graphs to show how amounts or percentages are distributed among a number of different items is the circle graph, sometimes called the "pie graph" because each amount is shown as a cut, or portion, of the whole "pie." To give yourself practice in reading this type of graph, look at the one above and answer these questions:

1. Which source contributes most to polluting our air each year? _____
What percentage of total air pollution is caused by this source? _____

2. The second and third largest contributors to air pollution are _____ and _____ .

3. The figures on this graph were obtained from government statistics. Why might the government keep such records? How might such a graph be used? Discuss with your classmates how this graph might interest an auto manufacturer, a factory owner, and a citizen in your community.

Reading Tables

Tables, or charts, are presentations of comparable facts. Unlike graphs, which rely on pictured symbols, tables are simply lists of facts. These facts, summarized in words or figures, are grouped under descriptive headings.

CHART

Worktime Required to Buy Food and Other Articles (1969)

Article	Amount	Average	Worktime Hrs.	Mins.
White flour	1 lb.	$ 0.15		2
Beef	1 lb.	$ 1.30		24
Fish	1 lb.	$ 0.77		14
Butter	1 lb.	$ 0.85		16
Eggs	1 doz.	$ 0.83		12
Sugar	1 lb.	$ 0.13		2
Man's suit	2 pc.	$ 79.30	24	29
Woman's skirt	1	$ 7.62	2	21
Man's shoes	1 pr.	$121.14	6	31
TV set	1	$141.09	43	33
Soap powder	20 oz.	$ 0.37		7

Look at the title of the chart above. It tells you the chart's purpose: to show the average worktime required to earn the money to buy certain common articles, based on 1969 wages and prices. Next, notice the headings of the four columns. The first column lists various foods and articles.

The second lists the amount of each article by quantity or weight. The third lists each article's price, based on average 1969 costs. The fourth lists the worktime required to earn the price of each article at average 1969 wages. For example, in 1969 a pound of white flour cost 15 cents. It took the average worker two minutes to earn that money.

Study the table; then answer the questions.

1. How much did a pound of sugar cost in 1969? _____

2. The item on this list for which you would have had to work longest is _____ .

3. For how many items would you have had to work more than one hour? _____ Which items are they? _____

4. Would it require more working time to earn the money for one pound of fish or for two dozen eggs? _____

5. Assuming an eight-hour working day, how many days would you have had to work to earn money for a TV set in 1969? _____

TIMETABLE

As we have seen earlier in this book, the skills you need for effective study are skills you'll use in many situations throughout your life. For example, when you travel by bus, train, or plane, you'll have to read timetables. Timetables, although they may *look* confusing, are just another kind of chart.

Below is an abbreviated railroad timetable. It shows trains running from New York City to Washington. The numbers at the far left (401, 101, and so on) are the numbers of the trains. At the bottom is a key that explains the symbols used in the table. You will have to study the key carefully to answer these questions:

New York—Washington

	New York, N.Y. (Penna. Sta.) Leave	Newark, N.J. Leave	Trenton, N.J. Leave	North Philadelphia, Pa. Leave	Philadelphia (Penn Central Sta.—30th St.) Leave	Wilmington, Del. Leave	Baltimore, Md. Arrive	Capital Beltway, Md. Arrive	Washington, D.C. Arrive	Equipment
△401 Mondays thru Fridays except July 5 and Sept. 6	—	—	—	—	7:10	7:40	8:48	—	9:40 AM	Coaches only
101 *Metroliner* Mondays thru Saturdays	6:30 AM	c 6:42	7:18	—	7:46	8:10	8:57	—	9:30 AM	Metroclub Car ★ Metro Snack Bar Coach
103 *Metroliner* Mondays thru Fridays except July 5 and Sept. 6, will also run July 3 and Sept. 4	7:30 AM	c 7:42	—	—	8:43	9:06	9:53	d10:17	10:30 AM	Metroclub Car ★ Metro Snack Bar Coach
133 Daily	8:00 AM	8:16	8:59	9:26	9:35	10:18	11:18	—	12:00 Noon	Parlor Club Car ★ Snack Bar Coach
105 *Metroliner* Daily	8:30 AM	c 8:42	9:18	—	9:46	10:10	10:57	—	11:30 AM	Metroclub Car ★ Metro Snack Bar Coach
135 Daily	9:30 AM	9:46	10:31	11:00	11:10	11:45	12:48	—	1:30 PM	Day Room Serv. Tavern Lge.
137 Daily	10:45 AM	11:01	11:45	12:12	12:21	12:51	1:51	—	2:40 PM	Parlor Club Car ★ Snack Bar Coach
107 *Metroliner* Daily	11:30 AM	c11:42	12:18	—	12:46	1:10	1:57	—	2:30 PM	Metroclub Car ★ Metro Snack Bar Coach
171 Daily	12:45 PM	1:01	1:46	2:13	2:22	2:53	3:58	d 4:27	4:45 PM	Parlor Club Car ★ Snack Bar Coach
109 *Metroliner* Daily	1:00 PM	c 1:12	—	—	2:13	2:36	3:23	d 3:47	4:00 PM	Metroclub Car ★ Metro Snack Bar Coach
163 Runs July 2, 5 and Sept. 3 and 6	1:55 PM	2:11	2:55	3:24	3:35	4:04	5:05	d 5:34	5:50 PM	Coaches only
143 Daily	z 2:10 PM	z 2:26	z 3:12	z 3:40	3:50	4:19	5:27	—	6:05 PM	Reserved Seat Coach
111 *Metroliner* Daily	2:55 PM	c 3:07	3:43	—	4:11	4:35	5:22	—	5:55 PM	Metroclub Car ★ Metro Snack Bar Coach

Reference Notes   c Stops only to receive passengers.   d Stops only to discharge passengers.
△ Train 401 also stops Chester 7:26 AM, Newark, Del. 7:51 AM and Aberdeen 8:17 AM.   n Stops Saturdays, Sundays and July 5 and Sept. 6.   z Stops to receive passengers for points South of Philadelphia

1. Suppose you take the Metroliner (105) from New York. At what time will you leave the station? _____ At which of the following stops will you be able to leave the train? (Underline the correct answers.) Newark, Trenton, North Philadelphia, Philadelphia, Wilmington, Baltimore, Capital Beltway, Washington.

2. If you want to leave New York as early as possible on a Sunday morning, you'll take the _____, which leaves at _____. You'll arrive in Washington at _____. How many hours will the trip take? _____ Can you buy something to eat on the train? _____

3. If you want to leave New York as close as possible to 11 A.M. and arrive in Washington before 3 P.M., you will take the _____. Would this be the fastest and most convenient train to take at about that time of day? Explain.

4. A close study of this timetable shows that the fastest trains between New York and Washington are called _____. At what hours do they leave New York? _____

Reading Pictures

Finally, we're back at the beginning of this chapter—with a picture. Pictures—including photographs and cartoons—are among the most common visuals used in books, newspapers, magazines, and reference materials. Usually the picture illustrates an important or interesting point in the accompanying text. As you read pictures, watch for the following:

• **Title.** The title of a photo or cartoon—usually just a short phrase—suggests the subject of the picture and, sometimes, the writer's attitudes toward what is shown.

• **Caption.** A caption goes further than the title in giving information to help you understand the picture. The caption of a photograph, for example, may tell where and when it was taken. It may also indicate the point in the accompanying text to which the photo relates.

• **Credit.** A picture's credit line is usually printed in very small type at one side. It tells to whom the picture belongs and, in many cases, who produced it.

• **An opinion.** Because pictures can present much information quickly and easily, they are often used to present a point of view. Sometimes only one side of a problem is shown. This is especially true of editorial cartoons. In studying pictures you should always ask yourself: Does this picture tell the whole story? Should I try to learn more about this subject before deciding how I feel about it?

Now, on to the pictures!

PHOTOGRAPH

Interstate Highway 80 runs through some sparsely settled parts of Pennsylvania where interchanges are often ten miles apart. An ad pointed out that 370 roadside emergency telephones along this 95-mile stretch of road are helping to make this section one of the safest highways in the state.

1. What is the title of this photo? _____

2. Suppose you had not read the caption. What might you think the photo showed? What would you have thought about the car? _____ Why? About the road? _____ About the man? _____

3. What do you think is the key word in the caption? _____ Why? What does this word suggest about the circumstances under which the photo was taken? _____

4. If there had been no caption, would the credit line have helped you figure out the photo's purpose? _____

CARTOON

Drawing by Frascino; © 1968
The New Yorker Magazine, Inc.

1. Does this cartoon have a title? _____ Does it have a disguised title? _____

2. What is the setting of this cartoon? _____ _____ Do you think it's meant to show the past? present? future? _____

3. Do you think the cartoonist believes this is a realistic scene? If not, why did he draw it? _____

4. Circle the word that most nearly describes the artist as we know him through this cartoon.
conservationist   motorist   road builder

forest ranger

More Things to Do

1. Look through a current daily newspaper. What visuals can you find? Can you read them quickly and easily?

2. How well do you think each is presented? Do the maps have a scale of miles and a directional indicator? Are the graphs and charts clear? Are their titles really descriptive?

3. Everyone in the class should bring in a photo with neither title nor caption. Exchange

photos; then write down your impressions, in just a few words or phrases, of the photo you have. Now ask the person who brought in the photo to check your impressions. How close did you come to "reading" the photo correctly? Did the lack of title and caption keep you from understanding it?

4. Is it possible for you to find two newspapers with opposing views? If so, cut out a cartoon from each one on the same controversial issue. Write your comments about these cartoons. Answer such questions as these: With which cartoon do I agree? Why? Which cartoon attracts more attention? Which is more convincing? Which exaggerates more? Which is more original?

● **Answers** to exercises in this chapter:

Pages 50, 51: 1. The continental United States; toward the top. 2. 475; 1600 miles. 4. Mississippi, St. Lawrence; southward, northeastward; Appalachian, Rocky. 5. 25°S, 47°N, 44°E, 125°W. 7. Denver.

Page 52: 1. Massachusetts. 2. East and slightly north; about 40 miles. 3. 90, because it looks wider than the others. 4. 9, 495, 20; no, because it's still under construction. 5. Woodville, Hopkinton, Marlboro, Watertown, Boston. 6. That Massachusetts is more heavily populated in the east than in the west.

Page 53, Bar: 1. Title. 2. Arabic, Bengali, etc.; alphabetically; 0 million to 600 million; the label "Millions of People." 3. Mandarin. 4. 190 million; 325 million; 190 million. 5. China.

Page 53, Line: 1. So that you can tell which line stands for which country. 2. 18,000; 500. 3. 1967. 4. 1955-60 and 1965-70; 1000 and 28,000.

Page 54, Line: Complex graph: 1. 40 percent; 5 percent. 2. It decreased slightly. 3. Transportation, etc., and professional and public service. 4.(a) No; (b) Yes.

Pages 54, 55, Circle: 1. Motor vehicles; 61 percent. 2. Factories, power plants. 3. Carbon monoxide; 1,600,000 tons. 4. Sulfur dioxode, oil and gas fumes.

Page 55: 1. 13c. 2. TV set. 3. 4; man's suit, woman's skirt, man's shoes. TV set. 4. Two dozen eggs. 5. About 5½ days.

Page 56: 1. 8:30 A.M.; Trenton, Philadelphia, Wilmington, Baltimore, Washington. 2. 133; 8 A.M.; noon; 4 hours; yes. 3. 137. 4. Metroliners; 6:30 A.M., 7:30 A.M., 8:30 A.M., 11:30 A.M., 1:00 P.M., 2:55 P.M.

Page 57, Photo: 1. Highway Help. 2. You might have thought the car broken, the road deserted, the man in trouble. 3. The word *ad;* that it was a posed shot. 4. It could have suggested that this was an ad.

Page 57, Cartoon: 1. No; yes, in the sign. 2. A superhighway; future, probably. 3. Probably to warn us of what the future might bring on an overcrowded planet. 4. Conservationist.

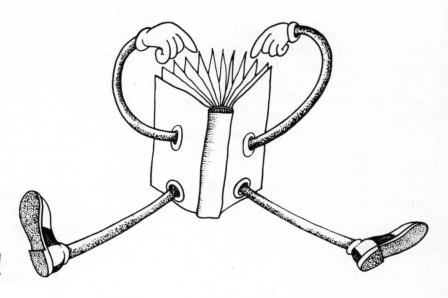

9·look it up!

Suppose that in studying you come across a word whose meaning you don't know. Or an explanation you don't understand. Or mention of a current news event you've never heard of. If your reaction to something unknown is to "skip it," you'll have to skip it as far as being a good student is concerned, too. A good student looks up words, facts, and figures he doesn't understand. Furthermore, a good student knows—

- how to use the different parts of a textbook or other reference work;
- what his dictionary can tell about words;
- how newpapers, magazines, and radio and TV programs help in learning;
- how visits or letters to industrial, business, and historical places can help him get facts, figures, and other information.

After reading this chapter, you'll know too!

Use Books More Efficiently

To enjoy a novel, you just glance at the jacket —and start reading. In reading or studying a textbook or reference work, however, you must know something about its principal parts— the title page, the copyright page, the table of contents, the author's introduction, the index, and the appendix. You'll find that *each* part helps you learn from the book.

The title page gives the title of the book, the author's name and usually his position, the publisher's name and address, and sometimes a printing or publishing date.

The copyright is usually printed on the back of the title page. This page gives the year the book was copyrighted—that is, when the publisher obtained the exclusive right to publish the book. It may also give a year when the book was revised—that is, its contents brought up to date.

The author's preface usually tells briefly what the book is about. It may also explain the purpose of the book and describe the methods and materials used in writing it.

The table of contents lists in order of appearance the titles of the chapters and the number of the page on which each chapter begins. This table may also list the main headings within the chapters.

The list of illustrations gives the title and page number of each map or other illustration in the book. With this list you can easily and quickly find a specific illustration.

The main part of the book contains, chapter by chapter, the detailed subject matter.

The footnotes at the bottom of some pages may give the titles of books and other sources of information the author used, explain some of the points in greater detail, or refer you to other pages or parts of the book.

The appendix contains additional information related to the book as a whole or to certain chapters. This information is often in the form of tables, maps, or charts.

The glossary explains technical words or terms used in the book.

The bibliography may appear part by part at the end of each chapter, or as a whole near the end of the book. The bibliography lists books, pamphlets, and magazines the author used as sources of information. They are also sources of further information for you.

The index is an alphabetical list of the topics presented in the book in addition to the page numbers on which these topics appear. The index of a history book, for example, may have such an entry as this: *Twenty-sixth Amendment, 12ff., 132, 215, 291ff., 367.*

The first reference, *12ff.,* means page 12 and several pages that follow. By looking up all the listed pages, you can quickly find all the information the book contains about the Twenty-sixth Amendment.

An Exercise

Using your history textbook, fill in the following blanks:

1. Title _____

2. Author _____

3. Publisher _____

4. Date of copyright _____

5. Does the book have an author's introduction or preface? _____

6. The index appears on pages _____ to _____.

7. Does the book have an appendix? _____

The Main Parts of a Book

Directions: In the test that follows, match list I and list II. Read sentence 1. Find the part of the book that correctly completes this sentence. Do each of the other sentences in the same way.

List I – The Book Parts

appendix	index
bibliography	preface
copyright page	table of contents
footnotes	title page
glossary	

List II – The Sentences

1. To find the year the book was published, consult the _____ or the _____

2. If you wish to read other references that relate to the subject matter of the book, consult the _____

3. If the book does not have an index, you may be able to find the reading material you want by consulting the _____

4. If you want to know the specific sources used by the author, look at the _____

5. To find the name of the company that published the book, consult the _____

6. For definitions of terms used in the book, consult the _____

7. You can quickly determine whether and where a book contains the specific information you need by looking in the _____

8. The author usually states his purpose in writing the book in the _____

9. To find the date when the book was last revised, or brought up to date, consult the _____

10. If you want to find tables or other important materials not included in the regular chapters of the book, consult the _____

11. The author's name and identification are shown on the _____ page.

Reading an Index

To give yourself practice in reading an index, match the items in the following two lists. List I is an excerpt from the index of a book. List II includes a number of topics that you might look up in the index. Read topic A in list II. In list I find the entry that applies to this topic. Write the page number or numbers of this entry in list II. Do the same for each topic in list II.

List I—The Index

FASHION
advertising, 190–194
artwork, 69–83
display, 49
    promotion, 51, 60,
        186–195
    stylist, advertising
        agency, 60
display work, 60
fashion director,
    186–195
Federal Trade
    Commission, 95
manufacturer,
    186–195
writer, 38, 58–68

List II—The Topics

A. fashion display_____
B. promotion of
    fashions_____
C. artwork on
    fashions_____
D. display work of
    stylist_____
E. writer on
    fashions_____
F. advertising
    fashions_____
G. director of
    fashions_____

Dictionary Use

Whether you use a paperback desk dictionary or an unabridged dictionary, you may not have realized how much information this reference work contains. For each word, a dictionary gives spelling, division into syllables, pronunciation, part or parts of speech, origin, definitions, and synonyms.

Here is the entry for the word *library,* from *Webster's Seventh New Collegiate Dictionary:*

li·brary \'lī-,brer-ē\ *n, often attrib* [ME, fr. ML *librarium,* fr. L, neut. of *librarius* of books, fr. *libr-, liber* book — more at LEAF] **1 a :** a place in which books, manuscripts, musical scores, or other literary and artistic materials are kept for use but not for sale **b :** a collection of literary or artistic materials (as books or prints) **c :** an institution for the custody or administration of such a collection **2 a :** a series of related books issued by a publisher **b :** a specialized collection of reference material; *specif* : MORGUE 2

The word *library* is a noun (n.). It achieved its present form in Middle English (ME), deriving from (fr.) the Medieval Latin (ML) *librarium,* and earlier from the Latin (L) *librarius,* meaning "of books," which derives, in turn, from the Latin *libr-,* or *liber,* meaning "book."

The entry gives five definitions of the word *library.* Thus *library* can mean a place in which books or other literary and artistic materials are kept for use; a collection of such materials; an institution that has charge of a collection of such materials; a series of related books; or a special collection of reference materials.

To help you pronounce words correctly, the dictionary has a section near the front called "A Guide to Pronunciation." The guide explains the pronunciation marks and symbols.

Abbreviations, such as those used for Old French, French, and Latin, are usually explained in the first pages of a dictionary.

GUIDE WORDS HELP YOU FIND WORDS

If your dictionary is *thumb-indexed,* use the letters of this index to turn immediately to the beginning of the section you want. If your word is *orange,* for instance, you find the index tab with the letter *O.* This tab is on the first page on which words starting with the letter *O* are found.

Now look at the guide words that appear at the top of the page. The guide word at the top of the left-hand column is the *first* word on the page. The guide word at the top of the right-hand column is the *last* word on the page. If you find a page headed *optimize* and *organ,* you know *orange* is somewhere on that page.

For practice in using the thumb index (if your dictionary has it) and guide words, see how rapidly you can find these words: *xylophone, cease, appetite, solitude, frantic.*

PRACTICE USING GUIDE WORDS

Match list I and list II below. List I gives some of the words that appear on pages 320–332 of *Webster's Seventh New Collegiate Dictionary.* List II gives the guide words that appear on those pages. Take the sample item *fragment.* This word belongs between the two guide words *four-poster* and *frame,* which appear on page 331. Therefore *fragment* is on page 331. In the same way, find the page number of each of the other words in list I, and write it on the blank line following the word.

List I	Page	Page	List II
O. fragment	331	322.	fluoride – flyover
A. forestry	_____	332.	frame – free
B. franc	_____	320.	float – flotation
C. forbid	_____	327.	forefeel – forethought-fulness
D. forget	_____		
E. fly	_____	323.	flypaper – foliar
F. food	_____	321.	flotilla – fluoridation
G. foam	_____	328.	foretime – formation
H. florist	_____	324.	foliate – fool
I. fossil	_____	326.	fora – forefather
J. flower	_____	330.	forty – four-o'clock

(Answers are at the end of the chapter.)

DICTIONARY EXERCISE

One by one, look up in your dictionary the words printed in italics below. Read the information carefully; then close your dictionary and underline each correct answer. When you've finished, open your dictionary and check.

1. *Colonnade* has how many syllables? (a) 1 (b) 3 (c) 4

2. *Colophon* is derived from what language? (a) Russian (b) French (c) Greek (d) Old English

3. What is the correct pronunciation of *cohesive*? (a) ko-'he-siv (b) ko-he-siv

4. The word *colony* has how many different meanings? (a) 1 (b) 2 (c) 3 (d) 4 (e) 7

5. *Colonial* can be used as either of two parts of speech (underline two answers): (a) adjective (b) noun (c) adverb (d) verb

6. A *seaplane* is most like (a) a helicopter, (b) a wheel, (c) a motorboat.

7. *Habit* comes from (a) Latin and French, (b) Old French and Latin, (c) Greek and Latin.

8. The *lachrymal* glands of the body produce (a) perspiration, (b) saliva, (c) tears.

Reading Newspapers

Do you read a newspaper every day? Do you know what kinds of information you can get from it? Here are the indexes of two typical daily newspapers—a small local newspaper and a big city one. Each index tells what departments are covered and where each can be found in the paper.

The Local Paper		The Big City Paper	
Amusements...14	Aviation..................43	Radio...........30
Bridge............11	Books 21	Real Estate...36
Classified 22	Business.................34	Screen.........19
Comics...........20	Buyers 35	Ships...........43
Deaths 17	Crossword Puzzle 21	Society 21
Editorial 16	Deaths, Obituaries...23	Sports..........27
Food 12	Editorials 22	Television.....30
Radio-TV 15	Fashions 26	Theater........19
Social............13	Food 26	Want Ads......43
Sports...........18	Music 19	Weather.......43

Many newspaper readers read only the headlines, the comics, and the sports or feature pages. If you want to get the most out of your newspaper, however, you should read all the important front-page news stories. Read also the editorials and columns that comment on the news. The editorials present opinions on news events. The columns give the "news behind the news" and usually present the writer's point of view as well.

It is a good idea to read at least two different newspapers from time to time, preferably papers that represent opposing points of view on controversial issues. Nearly every newspaper has a point of view. It is a good idea, therefore, to compare two local newspapers on the same day —their front-page news reports, editorials, editorial cartoons, and so on. As you read, ask yourself: In what ways are the two newspapers different in reporting the news? What are the differences in their editorial opinions?

The Sunday edition of a big-city paper will give you a great deal of information about topics you are studying. In the Sunday edition of the *New York Times,* for example, you can find excellent brief summaries of the news highlights of the week.

Your class may wish to purchase the Sunday edition of a city newspaper, not only for its news summary, but also for its book review section, magazine, and financial, travel, and entertainment sections.

On this checklist indicate with a pencil check mark how often you read each of the given sections of a newspaper:

	Always	Usually	Sometimes	Seldom	Never
News					
Drama, screen, book reviews, etc.					
Sports					
Comics, puzzles					
Editorial pages					
Financial news					
Society news					
Other					
Other					

Keep a record of your newspaper reading for a week and then enter a red check on the appropriate lines. Compare the two records. Are you reading more of your newspaper than you were a week ago? Which sections are you reading oftener than you did before? Is your newspaper reading helping you in school? How?

Using Magazines

You can draw on a large variety of magazines for information. For news about national and international events, you can read student magazines such as *American Observer* and *Senior Scholastic* and such publications as *Time, Newsweek,* and *U.S. News and World Report.* For articles on a variety of topics you can read *Life, Coronet,* or *Pageant.*

To find out more about what various magazines contain, spend some time browsing through them in your school or public library. List ten of these magazines and the titles of two major articles in each.

Using Radio and TV

You may listen to radio or TV as much as two or three hours a day. During most of this time you're probably tuned to entertainment programs—variety shows, popular singers and bands, sporting events, game shows, and movies. These programs may provide enjoyment and recreation.

Other radio and TV programs provide information about news events, scientific discoveries, new books, and other subjects. Form the habit of listening every day to one or more newscasters and news commentators. The newscasters give the news highlights of the day. The commentators usually describe one or two big news events, explain or comment on them, and tell you what they believe will happen next.

You can listen as the president of the United States and other prominent people make important speeches on the air. You can hear or see forums and panels on current topics. Often the participants on these programs are well-known public figures—congressmen, businessmen, scientists, artists. Such programs include "Meet the Press," "Face the Nation," and a host of programs on public and educational TV.

You can also learn from radio and TV dramatic programs. These may include plays by well-known playwrights or by outstanding but little-known authors. Some of the plays recreate historical events or dramatize famous novels.

CHECK RADIO AND TV LISTENING

Keep a record of your radio and TV programs for one week. At the top of the paper write the following headline:

MY WEEKLY RADIO AND TV RECORD

Day of Week	Time of Program	Name of Program
Sunday		
Monday		
Tuesday		
Wednesday		
Thursday		
Friday		
Saturday		

Each time you listen to a program, enter it in your record.

At the end of the week mark a check at the left of each program you think contributes to your schoolwork.

Make Visits to Learn

One of your best sources of information is on-the-spot visiting. For instance, if you are studying local government, your teacher may arrange a visit to the city hall or county building. If possible, talk with the mayor and the heads of various departments of government.

Either on your own or with your class, visit other places in or near your community to obtain information that will help you with your studies. You can learn at a museum, police court, hospital, factory, or telephone exchange, for example.

Before you make a local visit, draw up a plan. Your plan may include the following:

1. Talk with your teacher and parents about the visit you want to make.

2. Make the necessary arrangement, by letter or telephone, with an official of the place to be visited. Tell him the number in the group and agree on the best time for a visit.

3. Prepare a written list of the questions you want answered. Put the most important questions at the top of the list.

4. During the visit keep your eyes and ears open. Ask questions and make notes.

5. After the visit write a brief report that you can use later as necessary for your schoolwork.

Answers to exercises in this chapter:

Main Parts of a Book: 1—copyright page or title page; 2—bibliography; 3—table of contents; 4—footnotes; 5—title page; 6—glossary; 7—index; 8—preface; 9—copyright page; 10—appendix; 11—title page.

Reading an Index: A—49; B—51, 60, 186-195; C—69-83; D—60; E—38, 58-68; F—190-194; G—186-195.

Practice Using Guide Words: A—327; B—332; C—326; D—328; E—322; F—324; G—323; H—320; I—330; J—321.

Dictionary Exercise: 1—b; 2—c; 3—a; 4—e; 5—a, b; 6—a; 7—b; 8—c.

10 · off to the library!

Help! It's Tuesday. On Friday you have to report to the class on the history of United States–China relations. You must consult books, an encyclopedia, magazines, newspapers. Where will you find all these sources of information together? In the library, of course.

But do you know *where* in the library to find the titles of books on your subject? After you have the titles, do you know where in the library to get the books? Do you know where to find magazine articles on your subject? Do you know how to get the magazines in which the articles appear? Do you know where to find information on your subject in general reference books?

For your school library, the answers are probably *yes*. Most school libraries are relatively small and easy to find your way around in. The public library, however, is usually much larger, because it serves so many more people – people of all ages and with many different interests. If you live in a big city, the public library you go to may have several floors, a number of rooms, and what may seem at first a very complex arrangement for getting books or reference materials. You can learn, however, to use its card catalog, its guide to magazine articles, and its reference materials as readily as you now use a telephone directory.

To learn more about your library, find out how books and other printed materials are organized, or *classified*. Become familiar with the "finding aids," such as the card catalog. Find out how and where books and other printed materials are stored. Learn how to use encyclopedias and other reference books.

By becoming a better library user, you can quickly and easily obtain the book or magazine you're looking for. You can thus save time – both yours and the librarian's – and make the library a real help with your studies.

How Is the Library Organized?

In a typical public library, you first enter the general reading room. This large room is equipped with reading tables and chairs.

At one end of the room you'll find copies of current magazines and newspapers. These are displayed on tables, racks, or shelves. Back issues usually are bound and stored elsewhere in the building.

On shelves near the current issues of magazines you'll find volumes of the *Readers' Guide to Periodical Literature*. This guide helps you find magazine articles. Also in the general reading room are helpful reference books such as an unabridged dictionary, encyclopedias, atlases, and yearbooks. You use these books for different kinds of information. The books may not be taken from the library.

Near the entrance to the library is the desk to which you take books to check out and read at home. You also return books at this desk.

What Is the Card Catalog?

The library card catalog is probably in the general reading room. Use it to find the books you want. The card catalog is made up of hundreds of 3×5 cards stored alphabetically in the file drawers. Each card has information about a book – its title, author, subject, and call number.

For every book in the library there are at least three cards in the card catalog—the title card, the author card, and the subject card. On the title card, the first line gives the book's title—for example, *Our Federal Republic*. On the author card, the first line gives the author's name—for instance, *Judson, Harry Pratt*. On the subject card, the first line gives the subject of the book—for instance, *Federal government—States' rights*. For this book by Judson, the title card is filed under *O* for *Our;* the author card under *J* for *Judson;* and the subject card under *F* for *Federal government.* For books that deal with a variety of subjects there are several subject cards.

In the upper left-hand corner of each of the three cards is a call number. This number also appears on the book's spine—the part of the book that you see when it's on the shelf. This number guides you to the proper shelf.

How do you get a book?

First, go to the card catalog and find the call number of the book. *Second,* go to the shelves where books with similar call numbers are stored. *Third,* look at the call numbers of these books until you find the one you want. If you have trouble finding the book, ask the librarian for help.

The tiers, or rows, of shelves in a library are called *stacks.* Library books are arranged in the stacks according to the system of classification described below.

How Are Books Classified?

The librarian classifies books first into two main types: fiction and nonfiction. Each type is marked in a different way and stored separately from the other.

When the librarian receives a novel (fiction), he marks and stores it according to the author's last name. For example, to *Red Sky at Morning,* by Richard Bradford, he assigns a call number that starts with the letters *Br.* Can you tell why? He puts this call number on the spine of the book and on its three cards in the card catalog. Because the book is about a teen-ager growing up in New Mexico, the subject card is headed "New Mexico—Fiction." The book is placed on the proper fiction shelf.

The librarian in most public libraries employs the *Dewey Decimal Classification* to classify science, social studies, and other nonfiction. This system was devised by Melvin Dewey, a famous American librarian. Using the Dewey decimal system, the librarian assigns each book of nonfiction to one of ten main classes, as follows:

Range of Numbers	Nonfiction Classifications (with Examples)
000-099	Generalities (bibliographies, encyclopedias, periodicals, other general reference books)
100-199	Philosophy, psychology, logic, ethics
200-299	Religion (the Bible, other holy works), mythology
300-399	Social sciences (sociology, economics, law, public administration, education, commerce)
400-499	Language (languages, dictionaries, grammar)
500-599	Pure sciences (mathematics, astronomy, physics, chemistry, biology)
600-699	Technology, Applied sciences (medicine, engineering, agriculture, business)
700-799	The arts (architecture, sculpture, painting, music, recreation)
800-899	Literature (American, worldwide poetry, drama, essays)
900-999	History, travel, general biography

The librarian classifies each book of nonfiction according to these categories. He marks the call number of the book on its cards in the card catalog and on the spine of the book. If you know where the books in each nonfiction class are stored on shelves, you can go directly to them.

To check on your ability to classify nonfiction, read the list of subjects below. Then assign to each subject one of the ranges of class numbers presented above. For example, the range of classification numbers for a book on English history is 900-999.

_____A. English history   _____F. Geometry

_____B. German drama   _____G. Dictionary

_____C. Sports   _____H. American essays

_____D. Surgery   _____I. Psychology

_____E. Christian Science   _____J. Letter writing

Where Is the Book You Want?

All the cards are filed alphabetically in the card catalog drawers. Labels on the drawers show the part of the alphabet filed in each drawer. One drawer, for example, may be marked "A-B." All the cards giving a title, author, or subject that begins with *A* or *B* are filed in this drawer.

Suppose you're looking for a book on states' rights—that is, the rights belonging to the separate states of the United States. In the card catalog look under the heading "States' rights." The card with that heading reads, "*See* Federal government—States' rights." Now go to the "F" drawer of the catalog. There you find a number of subject cards headed "Federal government." Going through these cards, you come to one headed "Federal government—States' rights." On this card you see the call number of the book, the name of the author, and the title. These might be J923; Judson, Harry Pratt; and *Our Federal Republic*.

If you had known the author's name, you could have looked in the "J" drawer for *Judson*. If you had known the book's title, you could have looked in the "O" drawer for *Our*.

Here is a sample author card:

SAMPLE OF AN AUTHOR CARD IN THE LIBRARY CARD CATALOG

```
342.73

J923   Judson, Harry Pratt, 1849-1927
       Our federal republic. New York, Mac-
       millan Co., 1925, viii, 277 p.
       Bibliography, p. 271-274

Against the centralization of power as des-
troying the balance between federal and
state powers, which is the essence of our
Constitution.
```

As you read the catalog card for a book, copy some of the information on your own 3×5 index card. Record the book's call number, author, and title. If the library requires you to fill out a call slip, do so. To give yourself practice in making out an index card or a call slip (as follows) refer to the catalog card above for the Judson book:

SAMPLE OF A LIBRARY CALL SLIP FOR A BOOK

```
LIBRARY CALL SLIP

Call Number              Author
_____          _____
Title_____
Your name_____
Your address_____
```

As you read an author card you should also understand the other information given. To check your ability to do this, look again at the sample author card and answer these questions:

1. Who published this book? _____

2. When was the book copyrighted?
   _____

3. How many pages are there in the book?
   _____

4. How many pages are there in the bibliography? _____

5. The author was born in _____ and died in _____.

Most public and high school libraries use the Dewey decimal system of classifying and cataloging books. The Library of Congress and some other very large libraries, however, use another system. Whatever the library's classification system, you may follow these simple rules:

1. Use the card catalog to find the call number of the book you want. Do this by looking under the author's name, the book title, or the subject.

2. On a 3×5 card or a library call slip write the book's call number, author, and title. Using the call number, go to the proper library shelf in the stacks and get the book or hand the card or slip to the librarian, who will get the book for you.

3. If the library does not have a copy of the book or if its copy has been checked out by someone else, ask the librarian for assistance. He will be glad to suggest other books on the subject

you're studying or will put your name on the waiting list for a book you really must have.

To give yourself further practice in using a large card catalog, match list I and list II below. For example, the subject "Peanuts" will be in the drawer labeled "PAU–PER." For each of the subjects find and write in the correct drawer number.

No.	Ltrs.	Key Ltrs.	Subject	Drawer No.
1.			Peanuts	1
1.	PAU–PER	A.	Postal Service	___
2.	PES–PH	B.	*Pride and Prejudice*	___
3.	PI–PN	C.	*Pillars of Society*	___
4.	PO–PORTN	D.	Quito	___
5.	PORTO–PRE	E.	Real estate	___
6.	PRI–PROG	F.	Religion	___
7.	PROH–PSYCH	G.	Reykjavik	___
8.	PUB–REAC	H.	Revolution	___
9.	READ–REI	I.	Philippine Islands	___
10.	REJ–REZ	J.	Photography	___

Standard Reference Books

One section of the library is devoted to reference books—encyclopedias, dictionaries, almanacs, yearbooks, and atlases. These books are usually kept in the general reading room, where anyone may consult them for information. They provide facts and figures on just about every subject.

To learn about these reference books, spend an hour or so examining them. Leaf through a few to discover what they contain. Some will have illustrations and indexes you will want to look at.

Encyclopedias. If you want information on ecology, gravity, nuclear energy, or almost any other topic, you'll find it in a general encyclopedia. In such an encyclopedia you can read articles (illustrated with graphs, charts, or pictures) on agriculture, religion, arts, crafts, business, government, and so on and on.

Each article in an encyclopedia has been written or checked by an expert in that field.

You may expect to find all the important facts that can fit in the space available.

When you use an encyclopedia, look at its *latest* copyright date. If you are studying a topic such as the H-bomb or space development, you should first read the article in a recent edition of an encyclopedia. Then read an article on the same topic in the encyclopedia's most recent annual supplement, or *yearbook,* if there is one. Finally, you should read articles on the topic in current magazines, newspapers, and books. On a topic in which there are constant new developments, the encyclopedia may provide excellent *background* information, but not *current* information.

In looking up a topic in an encyclopedia, you should of course use its index. This may be in a separate index volume. In some encyclopedias each volume has its own index at the end. In others the index takes the form of cross references throughout the set. (For example, you are looking for "East Pakistan." The entry reads "East Pakistan. *See* Pakistan.") No matter where the index appears, however, it will be in alphabetical order, to make it quick and easy to use.

Which Encyclopedias Are Available?

Encyclopaedia Britannica is the most famous of all encyclopedias in the English language. First published in the years 1768-71, it is also the oldest. It contains scholarly articles on all general topics. It has an annual supplement, *Britannica Book of the Year.*

Encyclopedia Americana covers all subjects. It is especially strong in science, technology, government, and business. Its annual supplement is *Americana Annual.*

In addition to these reference works, you might use *Compton's Pictured Encyclopedia* and the *World Book Encyclopedia.* For special information, you might consult such sources as the *Encyclopedia of the Social Sciences* and *McGraw-Hill Encyclopedia of Science and Technology.*

Which Volume Do You Want?

In a multivolume encyclopedia, the spine of each volume has guide letters to help the reader find a particular topic.

The *Encyclopaedia Britannica* uses *guide words* on the spine of each volume. Volume 1 of the 1971 edition is labeled "A–Anstey." Suppose you want information on kangaroos. Look first in the index volume—volume 24. There you find the entry: "KANGAROO 13–205c; 14–972c. Austr. 2–7836b; brain 4–73c," and so on. The first general article on the kangaroo appears in volume 13, page 205, beginning in the top half of column 2 (*a* after the page numbers means the upper half of column 1, *b* means the lower half; *c* means the upper half of column 2, *d* means the lower half).

Although you would usually use the index to find something in the *Encyclopaedia Britannica*, you can find many important topics by using the guide words only. To test your ability to use these guides, match list I and list II below. For example, suppose you want an article on France. This will be found in volume 9—"Extradition–Garrick." At the right of each of the titles below write the number of the volume in which it appears:

	List I		List II	Answer
Vol.	Guide Words		Key Title	Vol. Number
1	A–Anstey	A.	English History	_____
2	Ant–Balfe	B.	Child Psychology	_____
3	Balfour–Both	C.	Glass	_____
4	Botha–Carthage	D.	Australia	_____
5	Carthusians–Cockroft	E.	Diesel Engine	_____
6	Cocker–Dais	F.	Crete	_____
7	Daisy–Educational	G.	Paul Bunyan	_____
8	Edward–Extract	H.	Germany	_____
9	Extradition–Garrick	I.	Bison	_____
10	Garrison–Halibut	J.	Fluorine	_____

Other Reference Works

You may find it necessary to consult other kinds of references—references that will help you get more up-to-date or more nearly complete information on topics in your subject areas.
Statesman's Year Book, published annually, supplies information about countries of the world.
World Almanac provides yearly information, including statistics, on many topics.

Information Please Almanac provides yearly information, including statistics, on many topics.
New York Times Encyclopedic Almanac, an annual published for the first time in 1971, provides in-depth articles by authorities in many fields, as well as facts and statistics.
Statistical Abstract of the United States, published yearly, gives figures on population, production, education, and the like.
Columbia Lippincott Gazetteer of the World lists and briefly describes nearly every geographic location in the world.

To get acquainted with these reference books, take time to look quickly through each one. Skim the table of contents and the index to get an idea of what the book contains.

How Well Can You Select Sources of Information?

In which reference work or works will you find each topic listed in list II? Mark the answers.

List I—References		List II—Topics
A. Dictionary	_____	1. Population of Ohio in 1970
B. Encyclopedia	_____	2. Theodore Roosevelt
C. *World Almanac*	_____	3. Pronunciation of *demitasse*
D. *Dictionary of American Biography*	_____	4. Article on coal
	_____	5. Louisiana Purchase
E. *Statesman's Year Book*	_____	6. Greek culture
F. World Gazetteer	_____	7. Recent Olympic champions
	_____	8. Exact location of Whitefish Bay, Wis.
	_____	9. Lewis and Clark expedition
	_____	10. The name of the governor of Hong Kong

More Suggestions for Using Reference Works

1. If you want recent information, look at the copyright date. If there are several copyright dates, the latest is the one that counts for your purposes. Dates of *printings* do not matter.

2. If you're unfamiliar with the reference work, glance at the table of contents to see what topics it covers.

3. To find the page or pages on which your topic is discussed, use the index.

4. If you have any questions about reference books, ask your teacher or librarian for help.

Use Magazines, Too

Do you want to find recent magazine articles on China, the United Nations, nuclear energy, electronic advances, or any other topic? If so, use the *Readers' Guide to Periodical Literature* (*Readers' Guide* for short).

Readers' Guide is an alphabetical index to articles published during a certain period of time in a great number of popular magazines. Each article is indexed under its subject or subjects and also under the author's name.

If you are writing a report on some current event in science or world affairs, you will certainly use *Readers' Guide*. The monthly and annual issues of this reference work are usually on the shelves in the library's general reading room. If not, ask the librarian for it.

Suppose you're writing an article about phonograph records. In *Readers' Guide,* look first for the subject heading "Phonograph Records." Under that heading you'll find a number of entries. One appears here:

Records: summer's choice.
il Time 98:53 Ag 30 '71

This entry presents the title of the article: "Summer's Choice." It does not give the author's name. Next, the entry indicates that the article has illustrations (il). Then it gives the name of the magazine (*Time*); the volume number (98); the page number (53); and the issue date (August 30, 1971).

To save space and to include as many entries as possible, *Readers' Guide* abbreviates the names of most magazines. These names and their abbreviations appear on the introductory page of each volume of the guide. Some examples: Am Ed—*American Education;* Bsns W—*Business Week;* Cur Hist—*Current History.* Such abbreviations as *il, m,* and *w* stand respectively for *illustrated, monthly,* and *weekly. Ja, F, Mr, Ap,* and so on, stand for the months.

Some entries in *Readers' Guide* are author entries. Here is part of an author entry:

REED, William F. jr
All business for the Big Bird. il Sports Illus 35:14-15 Ag 23 '71
Queen of the divers is King. il por [portrait] Sports Illus 35:31-3 Ag 16 '71

Under the name of the author are the titles of the articles he wrote and then the names, volume and page numbers, and issue dates of the magazines in which the articles appeared.

To check your ability to use *Readers' Guide,* study the sample entry below. Then answer the questions that follow.

PHONOGRAPH records

Recordings. R. Jacobson. Sat R 54:58 F 27; 58 Ap 24: 51 Je 26: 50 Ag 28 '71
Records: summer's choice. il Time 98:53 Ag 30 '71

Jazz music
Musical events: L. Armstrong. W. Balliett. New Yorker 47:75-7 Ag 28 '71

Music, Popular (songs, etc)
Music. D. Lupoff. Ramp Mag 10:61 S '71

Operas
Finally a Tippett opera. H. Weinstock. Sat R 54:52 Ag 28 '71

Passion Music
Recordings: Bach's St Matthew passion. M. Mayer. Esquire 76:26+ S '71

Piano music
New tales of Josef Hofmann. R. Jacobson il por Sat R 54:50 Ag 28 '71

Recording
New quadraphonic disc system. il Radio-Electr 42:2+ S '71

Rock music (songs, etc)
Dylan's New morning. R. D. Campbell. por Chr Cent 88:1009 Ag 25 '71
Pop E, Sander. Sat R 54:55 F 27; 75 + Mr 27; 57 Ap 24; 49 Je 26; 47 Ag 28 '71

1. In what magazine did the article "Finally a Tippett Opera" appear? _____ What volume? _____ What page? _____ What date? _____

2. Who wrote "New Tales of Josef Hofmann"?
_____

In what magazine did the article appear? _____
_____

3. In the entry under "Piano music," what does "il" stand for? _____

4. What article did W. Balliett write? _____
_____

After finding the entries in *Readers' Guide* for articles you want, copy all information given after the title on the call slips the library provides or on 3x5 cards. Put only one entry on each slip or card. Then follow this procedure:

1. Give them to the librarian; he will get the correct issues for you. Or, depending on the library rules, use the cards to get the magazines yourself from the stacks.

2. Skim the articles in the magazines quickly to see whether they have the information you need.

3. If an article has information of value to you, read it carefully. Make notes of interesting facts.

4. If you need assistance, ask the librarian.

Answers to exercises in this chapter:

Classifying books: A—900-999; B—800-899; C—600-699; D—600-699; E—200-299; F—500-599; G—000-099; H—800-899; I—100-199; J—600-699.

Author card: 1—Macmillan; 2—1925; 3—277; 4—4; 5—1849-1927.

Card catalog file drawers: A—5; B—6; C—3; D—8; E—9; F—10; G—10; H—10; I—2; J—2.

Encyclopedia volumes: A—8; B—5; C—10; D—2; E—7; F—6; G—4; H—10; I—3; J—9.

Selecting sources of information: 1—C; 2—B or D; 3—A; 4—B; 5—B; 6—B; 7—C; 8—F; 9—B; 10—E.

Readers' Guide: 1—Saturday Review, 54, 52, Aug. 28, 1971; 2—R. Jacobson, Saturday Review; 3—illustrated; 4—Musical events: L. Armstrong.

11: taking notes, making outlines!

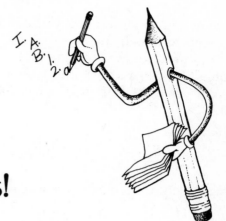

All right, you're back from the library, where you spent the afternoon researching a paper on, say, popular music of the 1960s and '70s. Now you sit down to think about your paper. I'll have a section on jazz, you tell yourself. Now, where did I read that fascinating article about Louis Armstrong? And what was the name of that book on the evolution of jazz? Darn, I'll have to go back to the library and check!

If this sort of thing has ever happened to you, you had better learn how to take good notes and make good outlines when necessary. Even if you have an excellent memory, you should take notes of things you may want to use later on. For example, always write down exactly what your homework assignments are. Make written notes about any reference materials you're reading for classroom reports, themes, or tests. Jot down notes on important points made by your teachers or by assembly speakers. Notes will help you remember the most important things about places you visit or people you interview. Only by taking notes can you recall, accurately and in detail, what you read, see, and hear.

Use your notes to make an outline for a talk or a written composition. This is something all experienced writers and speakers do.

Notes are both a record of significant facts and an aid to remembering them. They help you distinguish the essential facts from the non-essential ones. They also help you organize your facts into a clear and logical outline for writing or speaking.

What Materials Do You Need for Notetaking?

You can of course write your notes on the back of an envelope or on any other scrap of paper. That's fine in an emergency when you have no other paper with you. If you want good notes, however, you should record them in a notebook.

Your notebook should be large enough to allow you to write clearly and legibly. If it is too small, you may have trouble both in recording notes and in reading them later. Sheets that measure 8½ by 11 inches are the most practical size.

If you use a *loose-leaf* notebook, you have the added advantage that you can easily add blank pages where you need them. Also, you can easily take out all the pages and reorganize them as necessary. Because this kind of notebook is so flexible, you can keep it well organized by subjects of study. You can also keep it up to date by putting in new pages and taking out old pages.

If you're taking notes you'll need for only a day or two, you can make them in pencil. If you're writing them for much later references, it's better to record them in ink.

Should I Use Shorthand?

You can use shorthand in taking notes. If you haven't taken a course in standard shorthand, you can develop your own system. For example, you can omit such words as *a, an,* and *the* because they're not essential to what you're recording. You can leave out the vowel sounds and write down the consonant sounds—for example, *hs* for *house.* Some other abbreviations you may use:

abt—about	n—no, not, nor, neither
b—be	r—are
bf—before	shd—should

As you become more skilled in developing and

using your own system, you can also leave off many word endings.

For practice in inventing and using abbreviations, look at each of the words below. At the right of each, write a possible abbreviation for it.

education _____   miscellaneous _____

manufacture _____   magazine _____

different _____   month _____

distance _____   liberty _____

great _____   information _____

Your answers might be *edu, mfr, diff, dist, grt, misc, mag, mo, libty, info;* or you may have thought of abbreviations that make more sense to *you.*

What Kinds of Notes Should You Take?

If you are reading *your own* book, you can make notes directly in it by underlining important statements or by writing comments in the margins of the pages.

Underlining is the simplest form of note-taking, but it has an important disadvantage. When you underline, you are in a sense copying the author's words. You are not restating in your own words what the author wrote, and thus you may fail to understand it thoroughly.

However you take notes, bear in mind these suggestions:

- When you take notes on what you read, hear, or see, *record only the more important ideas.*
- Write notes that give you *clues to the main facts or ideas* you may want to use later.
- *Don't write down too many details.*
- *Copy something word for word only if you wish to quote it later.*
- To save time and effort, *record your notes as words or phrases instead of as complete sentences.*

Here, in outline form, are organized, edited notes on a magazine article:

I. The United Nations' role in the world today
   A. Peace keeping
      1. Help settle border disputes
      2. Arbitrate territorial claims—ocean, space, etc.
      3. Provide meeting place for nations
   B. Help for underdeveloped nations
      1. Education
      2. Health care
      3. Vocational training
   C. Objections to UN
      1. Too expensive
      2. Ineffective
      3. Interferes too much in national affairs
   D. Possible UN future role
      1. Help build world government
      2. End world hunger
      3. Promote just distribution of world's goods

When you're reading a book chapter or a magazine article, taking notes in outline form such as this is simplified because you have the author's work to refer to as you make your outline.

You may be able to take notes in outline form while listening to a lecture, discussion, or interview. If the speaker presents his ideas clearly and logically, he may give you such clues as "The first step..." or "The second reason..." These clues help you organize your notes as you go along.

What if a speaker's talk is poorly organized? Then you must listen for and record his ideas one after the other as he gives them. You'll have to wait until later to organize them yourself.

Edit Your Notes

Most notes need editing—correcting and organizing—to put them into the best possible form. Here's how to go about the job:

1. Soon after you record your notes, read them carefully and make changes or corrections.
   a) Be sure each note is worded so clearly that it can be understood by other readers as well as yourself.
   b) Add important points you may have omitted.
   c) Cross out points that are not essential.

2. Put your notes in outline form so that the major points stand out and minor points appear under the appropriate major points.

3. At the end of the outline write a brief summary in your own words.

A day or two after you have edited and outlined your notes, review them thoroughly. After that, review them once or twice a week to refresh your memory.

Before a test, review the notes that cover the material on which you are to be tested. This will give you the important ideas quickly, accurately, and completely.

Organizing an Outline

In an outline you present ideas from your notes in an organized form. Such an outline is like a blueprint. It shows a plan—as a whole and part by part.

To prepare an outline, review the ideas you have read or heard and have developed on your own. Then organize these ideas in outline form.

Your outline shows the flow of ideas and the relation between them. It also shows their relative importance—the major ones, and the minor ones that support or explain the major ones. In the outline's summary indicate what these ideas add up to—the conclusions you draw from them.

There are two main kinds of outlines—the *phrase outline* and the *sentence outline*. Partial examples of each type follow.

Phrase Outline
1. Inca civilization
   A. Rise of the Inca empire
      1. Conquest of western South America
      2. Progressive nature of Inca rule
         a) Roads, canals, aqueducts built
         b) Farming, weaving, crafts taught
         c) Work for common good, according to ability

Sentence Outline
1. The Incas had a highly developed civilization.
   A. After the Spaniards came to America, the power of the Incas declined.
      1. The Spaniards invaded and conquered Peru.
         a) They looted the wealth of the Incas.
         b) They ruled by treachery.

As the two examples show, the two kinds of outline have the same general form. The major ideas in each are written to start farthest at the left on a page. Minor ideas are indented toward the right.

Whichever kind of outline you use, be consistent. Make the outline either all phrases or all sentences. And remember—the examples above are only *partial*. In a complete outline you would never have a 1 without a 2, or an A without a B.

Practice Outlining

Next are four different topics—topic W, topic X, topic Y, and topic Z. Under topic W, six points are listed. Arrange these points in outline form. Write each point in the correct blank so that it is in the proper position in the outline. Organize the points for each of the other topics in the same way.

Topic W: Labor unions in the United States
1. Enactment of labor legislation
2. Origin and growth of labor unions
3. Safety laws enacted
4. Eight-hour day
5. Minimum wage
6. Wages-and-hours laws

I. _____

II. _____

    A. _____

        1. _____

        2. _____

    B. _____

Topic X: Moving to the city.
1. Many who move to cities expect glamor and excitement.
2. Many people go to cities seeking jobs.
3. Cities offer an abundance of entertainment places and restaurants.
4. Many jobless must go on welfare to survive.
5. Cities quickly become oversupplied with semiskilled workers.
6. Eventually, some people will give up and return to rural areas.
7. Cities are cultural centers.

I. _____

   A. _____

   B. _____

   C. _____

II. _____

   A. _____

   B. _____

Topic Y: China
1. Son remains home after marrying
2. The Great Wall of China
3. Curriculum difficult
4. Students in China
5. Used for protection
6. Few attend school
7. Extended 1500 miles along hills and valleys
8. Father is head of family
9. Chinese family life

I. _____

   A. _____

   B. _____

II. _____

   A. _____

   B. _____

III. _____

   A. _____

   B. _____

Topic Z: Need to conserve natural resources
1. Must be used wisely by industry
2. Needed for recreation
3. Tree farming
4. Retreat from urban U.S.
5. Purify water after industrial use
6. Swimming, boating, etc.

I. _____

   A. _____

   B. _____

II. _____

   A. _____

   B. _____

● **Answers** to exercises in this chapter:

Topic W: I−2; II−1; A−6; 1−5 (or 4); 2−4 (or 5); B−3.
Topic X: I−2; A−5; B−4; C−6; II−1; A−3 (or 7); B−7 (or 3).
Topic Y: I−2; A−7; B−5; II−9; A−8; B−1; III−4; A−3; B−6.
Topic Z: I−1; A−3 (or 5); B−5 (or 3); II−2; A−6 (or 4); B−4 (or 6).

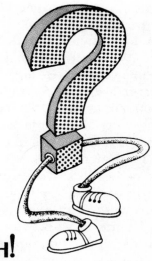

12·Think it Through!

Some things you just know are true—1 and 1 is 2; *B* follows *A* in the alphabet; maple leaves are green in summer; blue is the prettiest color.

Wait a minute! Is that last statement true? For you, it may be. But ask your classmates. They may prefer green, red, or yellow. It's all a matter of *opinion*.

In your studying you will come across many *facts*—Lincoln became president in 1861; the rule of the Russian czars ended in 1917. You will also come across many *opinions*—Lincoln was our greatest president; communism is bad. In order to really learn, it is vital to know how to tell the two apart. As you listen to a teacher or read a book, ask yourself, How can I find out if this is true? You must learn how to *evaluate*.

Much that we read and hear is difficult to evaluate. This is especially true of statements made by someone who is trying to make others accept his point of view on an issue. Some people question what he says; others do not. You may decide you don't know enough about the issue to judge what he says. If this is the case, you should check the accuracy of his statements *before* you evaluate them.

Interpreting Facts

Suppose you read about a single event in two different newspapers. The facts may be the same but the interpretation may differ. Consider these conflicting accounts of a theft:

In newspaper A you read:

THIEF PANICS CROWD IN STORE

Blanktown, June 2—Customers at the Beehive Bakery were terrorized today by a man who snatched a loaf of bread and rammed his way through the crowded store. Thanks to the quick thinking of proprietor M. S. Little, who tripped an alarm, police from a passing squad car seized and jailed the fleeing man. He gave his name as John V. Jones, unemployed, and said he needed food for his family.

In newspaper B you read:

CONCERNED DAD THROWN IN JAIL

Blanktown, June 2—John V. Jones, whose children have gone hungry since he lost his job two days ago, walked into the Beehive Bakery this morning and grabbed a 30-cent loaf of bread from the counter. Proprietor M. S. Little sounded an alarm and a police officer nabbed Jones as he ran from the crowded store. Although the bread was recovered, the man was arrested on Little's complaint and jailed.

Both newspapers reported the following:

1. The date was June 2.
2. The man called himself John V. Jones.
3. The man entered the Beehive Bakery.
4. The man stole a loaf of bread.
5. The proprietor was M. S. Little.
6. The man was arrested by a policeman.
7. The man was put in jail.
8. The man was unemployed and had a family.

In each newspaper the writer used words that affected your attitude toward John Jones. The writer in newspaper A, for instance, implied with "gave his name as" that the intruder might be using an alias. With "said . . . he needed food for his family" he cast further doubt on the man's veracity. He also used the words *rammed, terrorized,* and *fleeing.* These prejudiced you against the man. The writer in newspaper B, however, used words such as *children, hungry,* and *30-cent loaf,* to make you sympathize with the intruder.

The headline writers wrote heads appropriate to the stories. Headline writer A supported the story with *thief* and *panics.* Headline writer B had more to work with and used sympathetic words. Both considered what the reporter thought the important part of his story: for newspaper A, the theft and the customers; for newspaper B, the theft, the man, and his hungry children.

When different newspapers or news broadcasters agree on the essential facts about a person or an event, you can generally conclude that their reports are reasonably accurate. When they give different facts about the same event or interpret the same facts very differently, you wonder which is the more accurate story. This chapter will help you learn to examine carefully and thoughtfully what you read and hear.

Your Own Attitudes

In making evaluations you rely on your *feelings.* You probably believe, as the American Declaration of Independence states, that "all men are created equal." If so, you very likely show understanding toward people who differ from you in wealth, race, religion, and national background. You are friendly toward them and treat them with consideration.

By now you have acquired certain ready-made attitudes from your parents and friends. When you were small, your parents probably told you it was dangerous to play with matches and that fresh air and sunshine were good for you. Such attitudes were based on common sense and scientific knowledge.

As you grew older, you continued to accept many attitudes held by your parents and friends concerning behavior, politics, social questions, and other matters. Increasingly, however, you began to think about these yourself. You examined your attitudes—and changed some of them.

If you don't examine your beliefs occasionally, you tend to develop blind spots in your thinking.

You think you're always right. You can't see or understand another person's point of view.

Your Prejudices

Everyone has some prejudices. According to the dictionary, the word *prejudice* comes from two Latin words—*prae* meaning "before" and *judicium* meaning "judgment." If you *judge* someone or something *before* you have adequate information, you have a prejudice. This prejudice may be the result of complete ignorance or of only partial knowledge. Whatever the basis may be, prejudice usually prevents clear thinking and intelligent action.

You can improve your judgments of people and issues by noting the words, phrases, and ideas you are *for* and *against.* Take a few minutes right now to prepare two lists. In one, write down what you like—new clothes, parties, walking in the rain, good jokes, and so on. In the other list, write down what you dislike—thunder, Monday mornings, the color green, wearing a hat. After you complete these lists, ask yourself *why* you like or dislike each item.

Next mark each of the items in the list below. If you *like* it, mark it *L;* if you *dislike* it, mark it *D.*

_____ 1. Snakes	_____ 13. Dancing
_____ 2. Capitalism	_____ 14. Taxes
_____ 3. Going to church	_____ 15. Democrats
_____ 4. The draft	_____ 16. Farmers
_____ 5. Communism	_____ 17. Racial equality
_____ 6. Large crowds	_____ 18. Socialists
_____ 7. Politicians	_____ 19. Labor unions
_____ 8. Scientists	_____ 20. Divorce
_____ 9. Being alone	_____ 21. Lawyers
_____ 10. Germans	_____ 22. Landlords
_____ 11. Italians	_____ 23. Russians
_____ 12. Republicans	_____ 24. Daylight saving time

After you've marked the items on the list, discuss your responses with friends and family. Do they share many of your feelings? Compare the reasons they give for their feelings with your reasons.

Check on Your Prejudices

1. Try to understand yourself.
   a) Recognize your prejudices. One way is to

look over the list of things you dislike for little or no reason.

b) Realize that your prejudices affect the way you interpret information and the conclusions you come to.

2. Try to keep an open mind.

a) Read articles you disagree with as well as those you agree with.

b) Talk with and listen to people who disagree with you as well as those who agree with you.

c) Get as much information as you can from reliable sources.

d) Read and listen for facts as well as opinions.

Evaluate Your Sources of Information

In schoolwork your most common sources of information are teachers, textbooks, reference books, magazines, and newspapers. Your teachers are well informed in the subjects you're studying. Your textbooks were prepared by people who are regarded as experts in their fields. Teachers and textbooks are *relatively* free of prejudice. Keep in mind, however, that teachers and textbook writers are human beings — and that they may have prejudices they are hardly aware of. So listen and read *carefully.*

Because articles in many magazines and newspapers are written for popular reading, they usually contain less detail about a specific subject than do textbooks and reference books. All the facts may not be given to support every statement made or opinion expressed. Many articles are completely objective and fair, but others may be strongly biased — that is, prejudiced.

As a good student you won't swallow whole everything you read and hear. Instead, you'll think about and compare statements and opinions. You'll learn to recognize information that is presented from a biased point of view.

Check the Sources of Your Information

As you read or listen, consider carefully the sources of the information you receive. Some sources may be the following:

1. *Everybody says so.* Suppose you hear someone make the statement "Everybody says the United States will always be fighting a war somewhere in the world." If you hear such a statement, stop and think. Did the person who said it name the "everybody"? All "everybody says" statements are open to question.

2. *Tradition.* Suppose you read: "The three R's of reading, 'riting, and 'rithmetic were good enough for me. Therefore, they are all the education our children need today." The author of this statement is using tradition as his authority. The same author, however, would probably laugh if you suggested that to be consistent he should walk or ride horseback to work! There are no hard-and-fast rules on which is better, the old or the new. Some things have stood the test of changing times and proved their worth through the years. Others have given way to new needs and better methods, materials, and ideas.

3. *Experts.* When a true expert speaks, he is worth hearing. His statements are usually based on careful study.

For example, when a group of experts in the field of medicine announce a new finding after years of study and research, you can usually rely on it.

At one time smallpox caused many deaths each year. Dr. Edward Jenner, an English physician, after years of research, claimed that giving a person a light case of cowpox would make him immune to the more serious smallpox. He had observed that people who had contracted cowpox never contracted smallpox. At first other doctors, as well as the general public, disagreed with this theory, but in 1798 Dr. Jenner was able to prove he was right. His theory of *vaccination* became accepted medical practice.

In fields of specialization such as the natural sciences, the scientists themselves are usually the best sources of information about their fields.

Writers of books and magazine articles for the general public are not always themselves experts in the field they write about. If they are conscientious writers, however, they have gone to the experts for their source materials. It is not always easy for you to know how reliable your sources of information are, but you should try to find out something about them before you accept them.

Think Clearly

"The hand is quicker than the eye" is a familiar phrase among magicians who try to fool you with their clever tricks. "The word is quicker than the mind" might apply to the speaker who's trying to influence you to believe as he does.

Like a magician, a clever writer or speaker may use tricks to make you believe something that isn't true. If you're aware of such tricks, you are more likely to do the kind of thinking that will help you uncover the truth.

To think a problem through clearly, learn to distinguish between *facts* (what you really know to be true) and *assumptions* (what you suppose to be true).

Fact or Assumption?

Observers are likely to agree on the facts in a given situation, but they are less likely to agree on the *meaning* of those facts. For example, suppose you see your friend John clowning in class. You assume John is doing this to attract the attention of a girl friend. Another student assumes that John is doing it to annoy the teacher. Both you and the other student observe what John is doing, but each has his own *interpretation* of *why* John is behaving this way.

Both interpretations are *assumptions*. The real reason for John's showing off in class may be that he finds the work boring or difficult.

Opinions may be based on either *facts* or *assumptions*. To check your ability to distinguish between the two, read each statement below. If you believe a statement presents a fact, mark *F* on the line at the left of it. If you believe it presents an assumption, mark it *A*.

_____ 1. In the ideal form of government, the state is the servant of the people.

_____ 2. The result of dividing 25 by 5 is 5.

_____ 3. New York is the largest city in the United States.

_____ 4. In land area, Mexico is almost as large as our five biggest states combined.

_____ 5. The middle-aged worker is usually less efficient than the young worker.

_____ 6. Ill health, hunger, and poor housing are the concern not only of the individuals involved but of the entire community.

_____ 7. In the United States, more than 80 percent of the children between the ages of 5 and 17 are in school.

_____ 8. During the summer season in the Northern Hemisphere, the earth is farthest from the sun.

_____ 9. Under a world government, nations would have no reason to fight wars.

_____10. "The government that governs least, governs best."

Inductive Reasoning

If you say that someone "doesn't have a leg to stand on," it means someone has made a statement without having facts to support it. He may believe he is standing on solid ground, but in a manner of speaking, he is suspended in midair.

Almost everyone at times makes statements before collecting and examining all the facts. People frequently make general statements without thinking the matter through. You can learn to think logically by understanding what is meant by "reasoning."

What is *inductive* reasoning? When you reason inductively, you collect and study specific facts. From these facts you draw a conclusion.

Here is an example from science:

Inductive reasoning is sometimes called the scientific method. This method was employed by Copernicus, who in the 1500s developed the theory that the earth rotates on its axis and revolves around the sun.

For many centuries before Copernicus, astronomers believed in the theories of Ptolemy, a Greek astronomer who lived in Egypt during the second century A.D. According to the Ptolemaic theories, the earth was stationary at the center of all the heavenly bodies—that is, the earth stood still while the sun and planets revolved around it.

Ptolemy's beliefs were held by people generally. Then, as today, people saw the sun rise from the eastern horizon in the morning. They saw it move across the sky during the day and set into the western horizon in the evening. Common sense led them to believe, in view of what they saw, that the sun revolved around the earth. This belief was false, as Copernicus later proved.

Copernicus used scientific methods to investigate the solar system. He built crude astronomical instruments with which to observe the movements of heavenly bodies. He relied on mathematics, including geometry, to interpret his findings.

On the basis of his observations, computations, and comparisons, Copernicus developed and announced two highly important conclusions: first, that the earth turned on its axis, which explained why the sun appeared to go around the earth; second, that the earth, like the other planets, revolved around the sun — the center of our solar system.

Deductive Reasoning

In inductive reasoning, as we have seen, you collect a large number of specific facts; from these facts you draw a generalization. In *deductive* reasoning, you start with a broad statement, or generalization, that is assumed to be true; applying it to a specific case, you then reach a conclusion.

For example, the generalization that all humans are mortal is assumed to be true. No human has lived forever.

You can apply this generalization to the specific case of Jane Brown. Your deductive reasoning would run as follows:

a. All humans are mortal.
b. Jane Brown is human.
c. Jane Brown is mortal.

Taken together, these three statements are called a *syllogism*. The first statement in a syllogism is called the *major premise;* the second statement is the *minor premise;* and the third statement is the *conclusion.*

In both inductive and deductive reasoning, you must ask yourself, Is this statement true? true of some people or of all people? true in some events or in all events? What are the facts concerning this statement?

Detect Faults in Reasoning

It is important to be able to recognize certain kinds of faulty reasoning. Until you learn to detect such errors, you may be misled. Here are some of the more familiar types of faulty reasoning:

1. *Off to a wrong start.* If you accept a premise (the broad generalization) unquestioningly, you must also accept the conclusion that logically follows from this premise. For example, if you believe that "you can't change human nature," then you should logically believe that laws and rules of conduct are useless because people will never change to conform with them.

If the statement you start out with is false, or partly true and partly false, then the conclusion will be shaky. You may accept the premise "You can't wipe out poverty." Then you must conclude that many people will always live in misery. In this illustration, because the premise is partly true and partly false, the conclusion based on it is unsound. In your community, for instance, private companies and public agencies can take steps to reduce poverty and may even erase it completely.

To explain this kind of error more clearly, here are other examples in which the premise or the assumption is either completely false or partly false:

a. You get warts from touching toads. Therefore, you should never handle toads.

b. An apple a day keeps the doctor away. Therefore, if you eat apples regularly you will never have to see a physician.

c. The United States has nearly all the raw materials it needs and wants. Therefore, it can reduce or cut off trade with other countries.

2. *Guilt by association.* Sometimes people assume that because two things or groups of things have one characteristic in common, they are the same in all other respects too. You can come to some pretty ridiculous conclusions this way. For example:

a. Fish lay eggs.
b. Hens lay eggs.
c. Therefore, fish are hens.

This kind of reasoning can also lead to false conclusions that are not so obvious. For example:

a. Communists say they believe in peace.
b. She says she's for peace.
c. Therefore, she is a Communist.

3. *One robin doesn't make a summer.* At one time or other, most of us have heard people say such things as "You can't trust any of these

foreigners. I know, because one of them once worked for my brother and you couldn't trust him any farther than you can throw a piano." Carried to an extreme, this kind of argument could run something like this:

a. Mary is Greek.
b. Mary has weak ankles.
c. Therefore, all Greeks have weak ankles.

4. *The "so what" fact.* Sometimes you may make a judgment on the basis of information that is factual but irrelevant—unrelated to the main point. You may hear a speaker say, "Mr. Rojack will make an ideal mayor. He doesn't smoke or drink. He belongs to several civic clubs. His father was once mayor here."

The speaker gave you facts about Mr. Rojack, but they had very little to do with Mr. Rojack's qualifications for the office of mayor. The speaker failed to say anything about Mr. Rojack's experience or his ability to work with members of the city council. You don't know what his background is for administering the departments of city government or helping attract new businesses to the community.

To guard against inaccurate statements, be on the alert to identify irrelevant facts. Then you'll be more likely to make sound judgments based on facts that are important and related to the matter under consideration.

5. *Confused comparisons.* Some people are misled by a comparison of two things that are not really the same. This is a *false analogy.*

For example, you may describe a student as "slow but sure." It may be that if *you* want to do something as accurately and thoroughly as possible, you must do it slowly.

What is true for you, however, may not be true for *everyone.* For example, the student who is slowest in his schoolwork is not always the surest or the most accurate. Many good students are both fast *and* sure.

An analogy is an excellent way to describe a person, an object, or a situation, *if it is an accurate analogy and applies to the matter at hand.* A false analogy can be very misleading.

To explain an international problem, you may compare nations to persons. You may talk about a "family of nations" just as you talk about a "family of persons." This analogy is often helpful in gaining a better understanding of world problems. Yet it must be used with intelligence and care. You may say that a nation is "born," "grows up," "dies of old age," or is "killed by an enemy." You must recognize, though, that a nation is not a person and that when you speak of a nation you are speaking of many different kinds of people with different beliefs and ways of life.

6. *Going around in circles.* Another kind of error is sometimes called "thinking in circles." For example, you say, "John is a grind because he stays home every night and studies." You may also say that John stays home every night and studies because he's a grind. You haven't gotten very far! Another example: Some people say of the very poor that "they wouldn't know how to live better" even if they were given the opportunity to do so. Such people overlook the fact that without the opportunity, people can't begin to live better.

When you reason in a circle, you go round and round, each time returning to your starting point. Instead of giving evidence to prove your conclusion, you merely state it in another way. Or you give the *effect* or *result* of a situation and its *cause.* You make no progress; you don't move ahead in your thinking. The ultimate in circular reasoning is the hungry boy who declared, "If we had some ham, we could have ham and eggs, if we had some eggs."

7. *Words with whiskers.* A platitude is a dull, stale, commonplace statement. Usually it has been said over and over by so many people that unthinking individuals accept it as true. Examples: "Woman's place is in the home." "You can't keep a good man down." "Men think more logically than women." Avoid making such statements.

8. *What's the meaning of this?* Dictionaries generally agree on the meanings of words, but people may not. For instance, consider the meaning of the words *justice, democracy,* and *liberty.*

In 1860 many Americans agreed on what the word *liberty* meant—that is, the freedom or right to do as one pleases. More specifically, liberty meant the right of a person to come and go as he wished, to speak and write freely, and to hold private property. Yet there were arguments about its meaning. People who owned slaves or supported slavery wanted the liberty to buy, hold, manage, and sell other human beings as private property. People who opposed slavery, however, wanted the slaves to be free

—to have all the liberties of free men. Thus, the proslavery group and the antislavery group each had a different definition of liberty.

Today differing definitions of liberty may arise over the question of racially integrating neighborhoods in towns and cities. Some people claim the liberty to sell their homes only to people of their own race, to keep the neighborhood racially segregated. People of another race who want to move into the neighborhood say they have the right to live wherever they want and can afford to live. Obviously, both definitions of liberty can't exist in the same neighborhood.

9. *What's in a name?* A writer or speaker may use ridicule in his presentation to the public, but ridicule is often simply name calling. It seldom includes sound evidence for or against a person or a point of view.

The person who uses ridicule may not have the facts to back up his statements. He may be trying to cover up his ignorance or hide the real facts or issues.

Between Fact and Opinion

To check your ability to tell fact from opinion, mark each statement below either *F* (fact) or *O* (opinion).

_____ 1. In the depression of the 1930s the federal government established agencies to provide jobs for the unemployed.

_____ 2. If we keep taxes high, businessmen will be unable to make a profit.

_____ 3. If the government increases its help to needy people, they will lose their initiative and independence.

_____ 4. The government should close down any agency that has had cases of graft or other improper conduct.

_____ 5. In the United States a presidential election is held every four years.

_____ 6. The building of low-cost housing is the best way to improve the living conditions of the needy.

_____ 7. The average worker today receives much more income and works much shorter hours than the worker of 100 years ago.

_____ 8. Many people must be kept poor in order to maintain the wealth of a few.

_____ 9. Since 1900, machines have created more jobs than they have abolished.

_____ 10. Most of the federal government's yearly expenditures are for defense and for past and present wars.

_____ 11. The federal government should grant more money to the states so that they can help local districts build new school buildings.

_____ 12. Learning is not confined to a classroom; it continues throughout life.

Judge What You Read and Hear

In trying to become a better student you should not only gather information; you should also judge it. You should ask yourself: Is what I have read or heard accurate? complete? objective, or prejudiced?

In making judgments, remember that different people may notice different facts concerning the same person, object, or event and therefore arrive at different conclusions. Because of these differences, it is important to know whether your sources of information are reliable.

Learning to reason more clearly and to make sound judgments of people and things will help you in all your subjects of study — and throughout your life.

More Things to Do

1. Obtain reports on the same event from two different newspapers. Compare them and list the likenesses and differences. Mark each likeness and each difference *F* for fact or *O* for opinion.

2. Read editorials on the same subject in two newspapers that represent opposing points of view. Make a written list of statements in each editorial that reflect the opinions of that paper. Present them for class discussion.

3. Examine the following examples and check

to see whether the premises and conclusions are correct:

a. Civil disobedience always turns into violence. Jack believes in protest by civil disobedience. Therefore, Jack is violent.

b. All fish live in water. Scalawags are fish. Therefore, scalawags live in water.

● **Answers** to exercises in this chapter:

Fact or assumption?: 1—A; 2—F; 3—F; 4—F; 5—A; 6—A; 7—F; 8—F; 9—A; 10—A.
Between fact and opinion: 1—F; 2—O; 3—O; 4—O; 5—F; 6—O; 7—F; 8—O; 9—F; 10—F; 11—O; 12—F.
Premises and conclusions: a—False, because the major premise is untrue. b—False, because the minor premise is untrue.

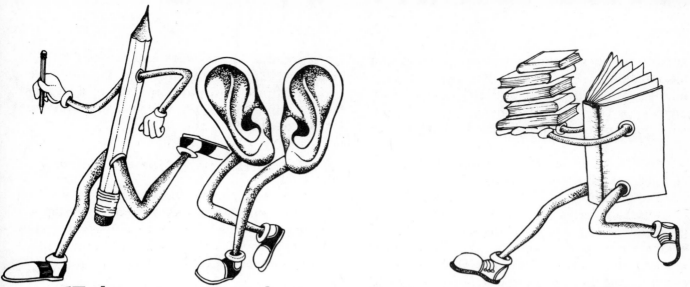

13 · How can you best participate in classwork?

What do you do during a class period? Do you sit silently like a bump on a log, or do you take an active part in class activities as a listener or a speaker? Do you allow your attention to wander from what is going on, or do you pay attention to what is being said or done? Are you noisy or thoughtless, or are you courteous and considerate toward the teacher and other students?

You are the only one who can answer these questions accurately. Only you can do something to improve your participation in class.

How to Participate More Actively in Classwork

If you take an active part in a class session, you'll learn more about the topic or subject you are studying. You'll also get greater satisfaction from it. Your teacher may take into account how much and how well you participate in classwork. You will gain the respect of your fellow students for your contributions to the class's activities. It pays to be active.

Too many students sit back and let others do all the talking during a class discussion. In fact, many students say they don't recite or participate in other ways because they lack preparation. Others say they don't participate because they hate to reveal how little they know, or are afraid other students will make fun of them. These are excuses. They must be overcome.

To improve their participation, such students should do their class assignments more conscientiously. They must conquer their doubts about what they can do and their fears about what other students think of them. This anyone can do with a little effort.

If you have carefully studied the material assigned, you'll have a good idea of the kinds of questions the teacher will ask—and you'll have the answers ready. If you know the answers, you'll participate more frequently and develop self-confidence.

During a class session your teacher may ask each student a question. If you have prepared for this session, you'll be able to give the answer when called on. When you answer, be brief and to the point.

Often your teacher will ask a question and ask that a student volunteer to answer it. If you know the answer, don't hesitate to volunteer.

When you volunteer to speak in class, you can offer information you've gained from the textbook, a reference book, or a recent issue of a newspaper or magazine. You can present facts, figures, or opinions you obtained from a radio or TV program, from a conversation with someone, or through firsthand observation. For example, your class may be discussing the Congress of the United States. If you have visited Washington, listened to a congressional debate, or talked with one of your congressmen or senators, tell your classmates about your experiences.

In addition, you may want to ask questions about the teacher's explanation of a topic or problem or about a student's report. When a question occurs to you, ask it at a convenient time—for example, just after the teacher has finished a presentation. Don't wait too long or fail to ask a question that seems important to you. If you do, the opportunity to get the answer will pass, and you may not take time to find out later.

When you want to make a comment, don't

hesitate to do so. State your point clearly and briefly. Whether you agree or disagree with what has been said, give your reasons, together with any supporting facts. Whenever possible, support your point by citing facts, figures, and sources.

At some time your class will undertake a special project, and you'll want to do your share toward planning it and carrying it out. Such participation helps you learn new things and gives you a feeling of achievement. It also gives evidence that you're a good student. Record your participation in class activities. On the accompanying checklist record your participation in the daily activities of one of your classes—an English class or a social studies class. If you answered a question correctly when the teacher called on you on Monday, mark a check at the right of activity 1 below the day, Monday.

Checklist of Your Participation in the Activities of a Class

ACTIVITY	M	T	W	Th	F
1. Answered the question the teacher asked me.					
2. Voluntarily answered a question the teacher asked the class.					
3. Voluntarily raised a question or made a comment during a class discussion.					
4. Expressed agreement or disagreement with another's opinion and gave reasons for doing so.					
5. Voluntarily made a special report to the class.					
6. Took an active part in a class project.					
7. Other activity.					

At the end of the week look at your filled-in checklist. Then write a few sentences in which you evaluate your participation and suggest ways to improve it. You will find space on page 90 for writing your sentences.

How to Participate More Effectively

A very large proportion of your class participation may consist in speaking and in working on committees. For this reason you'll want to consider the ways in which you can become more proficient in each of these abilities.

How to Speak Better

Do you mumble your words so that your teacher and other students can't understand what you're saying? Do you speak so softly that students sitting at the rear of the room can't hear you? In an oral report do you ramble and go off in different directions? Do you have to learn to speak better?

Whether you are answering the teacher's question, making a comment during a class discussion, giving a report to the class, or talking from the stage at a school assembly, you can learn to speak more effectively. To do so you must (1) think clearly, (2) speak distinctly, (3) use correct and appropriate language, and (4) talk in an interesting fashion.

1. *Think clearly.* If you study your subject and think about it before you speak, you're more likely to talk to the point, give the right answers, and win others to your side of an argument.

To think as clearly as possible about what you're going to say, prepare an outline. In the outline include the main points and, under each of these, the important minor points you want to cover in your talk. If you outline what you plan to say, you won't wander. You'll keep your speech on the track of your subject.

By knowing your subject and organizing beforehand, you're more likely to give a good speech that presents the material well and that your audience will like and enjoy.

2. *Speak distinctly.* Talk loud enough so that all students in the room can hear you. Say each word clearly so that your audience can readily understand you. Don't cut off the endings of words. If you're unsure about the pronunciation of a word, look it up in a dictionary.

3. *Use correct language.* Whether you're giving a short formal speech, presenting an informal report, or making a brief comment during a class discussion, try to use correct language. If you speak correctly, you're more likely to put your point across and make a favorable impression on your listeners.

If you want to be a good speaker, avoid making errors in grammar.

Here are some common errors you should be careful to avoid:

a) Subject and predicate do not agree.

Incorrect: The boys was at the game.
Correct: The boys were at the game.

b) Pronoun is in the wrong case.

Incorrect: It is him.
Correct: It is he.

c) Double negatives are used.

Incorrect: A good citizen never does nothing to
            hurt his country.
Correct: A good citizen never does anything to
            hurt his country.

d) A helping verb is omitted.

Incorrect: I done my report.
Correct: I have done my report.

e) A word is used in the wrong way.

Incorrect: Are you doing good in English?
Correct: Are you doing well in English?

You can learn to use correct language in your oral schoolwork in three ways: first, by studying carefully a textbook of English grammar; second, by looking up the meanings of words; and third, by asking your teacher to call oral mistakes to your attention.

As you give a speech, your teacher no doubt notes errors you make in pronunciation or grammar. Later, after the class has discussed your talk, you and your teacher can go over your errors so that you can avoid making them in the future.

To improve your speech, keep a notebook in which you record your errors in pronunciation or grammar as well as the correct form. By consulting your notebook from time to time, you'll learn to speak correctly.

4. *Speak in an interesting way.* If you are to be an effective speaker, you must get and hold the attention of your listeners. To do this, you must know your subject and be enthusiastic about it, for enthusiasm is usually contagious.

To add interest to your talk and to put across your points, include examples—that is, stories, anecdotes, or illustrations. Be sure, however, that every example helps you get your idea across.

During your talk avoid long lists of names, dates, and statistics. It is difficult for your listeners to keep this kind of information in mind when it is given orally, and they will lose interest in what you're saying.

In general, if you talk with enthusiasm, give examples, and concentrate on a few main ideas, your speech will interest your listeners and hold their attention.

To evaluate your effectiveness as a speaker, prepare and give an oral report to your class. After you present your report, answer the questions that appear next.

a) Did I organize or outline my talk in advance?

b) Did I stick to the subject of my talk?

c) Did I speak distinctly?

d) Did I enunciate clearly?

e) Did I pronounce words correctly?

f) Did I use language correctly?

g) Did I use the right words?

h) Did I feel and show enthusiasm for my subject?

i) Did I give one or more anecdotes or examples?

j) Did I avoid using long lists of names or figures?

Next, have another student answer the same questions about your talk. Compare your answers with his. On the basis of this comparison, decide on ways in which you can improve your public speaking.

The next time you listen to someone else speak, see what you can learn from him. Did the speech bore you or interest you? Why? Did your attention wander? If so, at what point? If you were speaking on the same topic, what changes would you make in the presentation?

Learn to Work with Others on Committees

As a student in a class, you are a member of a team. If your class is to succeed as a team, every student must do his part. This means that he must learn to work with others—for example, as a member of a student committee or a student panel.

Early in the school year your teacher will probably set up a number of committees in some of your subject classes. Each committee will have the job of carrying on a special project or investigating a special topic or problem. As a group, the class will make a list of the projects to be undertaken. Students who are interested in each project will then meet as a committee. They may elect a chairman and a secretary.

At its first session the committee should make certain that it understands its assignment—what it is to do. It also agrees on the duties of each member. The committee next discusses the possible sources of information and the problem that must be solved, and makes plans for the report it will give to the class. From then on each committee member does his part. He shares his findings with other members and cooperates with them in other ways.

From time to time the chairman of each project committee talks with the teacher. He reports on his committee's progress and obtains suggestions on what they are to do next. He reports these suggestions to his committee for consideration and action.

In conducting the work of his project committee, the chairman may take such steps as the following:

1. *Have committee members collect information.* After the committee has met once or twice, each member should investigate the part of the project for which he is responsible. He should carry on research by reading in the library, interviewing people, visiting places of interest, using other possible sources. During this time he should make notes that he can organize into a report (perhaps in outline form) for the committee.

2. *Have committee members pool their findings.* As the committee's work proceeds, each member contributes a report on the information he has gathered. The committee then examines each report and decides what information to include in its report to the class. Whether such a report will be oral or written, the committee should prepare it by using a carefully developed outline.

3. *Present the committee report to the class.* In a project report the committee members share their information and other findings with all other members of the class. Whether the report is oral or written, or both, the committee should do its best to make it interesting and informative. Whenever possible, committee members should have an opportunity to participate in presenting the report.

A checklist for committee work

Apply this checklist to a committee of which you are a member. At the right of each question mark a check to indicate whether your answer is yes or no.

A. Organization of your committee   Yes   No

1. Were members selected carefully with regard to their qualifications for the job? ___ ___
2. Has a chairman been chosen? ___ ___
3. Has a secretary (if necessary) been chosen? ___ ___
4. Was the subject for study clearly understood by members? ___ ___
5. Were parts of the subject for study defined? ___ ___

B. Responsibilities of a committee member

1. Did each member understand his duties? ___ ___
2. Did he consult reliable sources of information? ___ ___
3. Did he take adequate and helpful notes? ___ ___
4. Did he organize his notes as an outline? ___ ___
5. Did he make his information and other findings available to the committee? ___ ___

C. Report of the committee

1. If the report was a written one, did it meet the standards of good writing? ___ ___

2. If the report was oral, did the
   student who made the report
   a) speak clearly?　＿＿ ＿＿
   b) use correct English?　＿＿ ＿＿
   c) make the report interesting?　＿＿ ＿＿

Learn to Work with Others in a Panel Discussion

In a panel discussion a group of four or five students present a subject and discuss it. One of the students acts as chairman. He and the other panel members usually sit in front of the class around a table or in a semicircle.

The chairman opens the panel discussion by taking a few minutes to outline the subject. He calls on each panel member to present his ideas or point of view. Each member is allotted two or three minutes.

After all panel members have expressed their views, the chairman conducts a discussion among them. They engage in an informal give-and-take of facts and opinions.

Last, the chairman throws the discussion open to comments from the floor. At this time any student may ask a question of panel members, make a comment on what a panel member said, or express his own views.

If you have panel discussions in your classes, you may find these suggestions helpful:

1. Select a subject for discussion that is interesting to your fellow students, one that allows for real differences of opinion. Such a subject might be "What might be done to prevent war?" or "What should be the legal age for marriage?" If the subject interests many students, the discussion will be stimulating and challenging.

2. Have panel members meet in advance. At this meeting discuss and agree on the procedures for conducting the panel—for instance, the order in which the members will speak, the length of time, and so on. If these procedures are worked out beforehand, the presentation to the class will be more effective and interesting.

3. Choose a chairman who is skillful in leading discussions. The chairman himself should talk very little, but should encourage others to present their facts and opinions. At all times, the chairman should be tactful. He should keep panel members on the subject. He should discourage any student from speaking too often or too long, so that there will be enough time for students in the class to contribute to the discussion.

Be Considerate and Courteous

You can learn to work well with others by practicing certain commonsense rules of conduct.

1. Arrive at class on time or a few minutes early. By doing so you make it possible for the class to start on time without any distractions.

2. Do your share of the group work carried on by your class. Take an active part in preparing a committee report or conducting a panel discussion.

3. Be considerate of others. Pay close attention to what the teacher or another student is saying. Don't disturb other students by whispering or by attracting attention to yourself.

4. Meet your deadlines. Have your part of a committee report or panel discussion ready before it is due. If you are a chairman, be ready at least a day or two before the scheduled date.

5. Make every effort to be present in class on the day your group is scheduled to report. If you find in advance that you must be absent, inform your teacher so that he can make a change in the class program for that date.

If you follow these suggestions, you'll be more successful in your relationships with your teacher and fellow students. You'll also acquire skills and habits that will help you later in college and in a job. You'll develop a sense of personal and social responsibility that will benefit you in many ways.

More Things to Do

1. Try to take a more active part in classwork. Volunteer as a member of a project committee or discussion panel or give a special report on a topic related to what you are studying.

2. After your committee has presented its

report or your panel has given its discussion, get together to evaluate the results.

	Yes	No
1. Was each member prepared?	_____	_____
2. Did each member contribute?	_____	_____
3. Were members considerate of one another?	_____	_____

4. Did any member take up too much time? _____ _____
5. Did the chairman make sure each member had a chance to speak? _____ _____
6. Did the chairman encourage comments from the class? _____ _____

Discuss ways in which your committee or panel could have improved its presentation.

14 • how can you best prepare for and take tests?

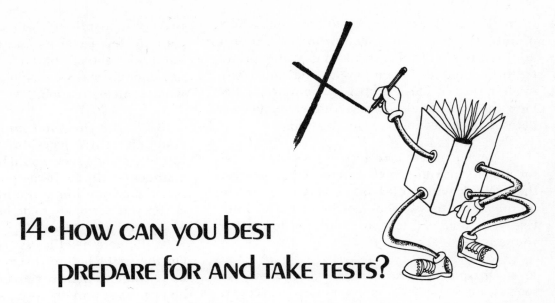

Tests provide information about what you have learned—information that can be obtained in no other way.

Tests are valuable aids to your present education. They also help you prepare for your later years in high school, for college, or for a job after you leave high school.

When Do You Take Tests?

You will have many tests while you are in school. You may take special tests to get into college. If you go to college, you'll take many tests before you graduate.

After you finish high school or college, you may face additional tests. If you apply for a job in business, you may be given general aptitude tests and tests of particular skills, such as typing and shorthand. If you go into military service, you will take tests of general mental ability and specific aptitudes or skills. If you apply for a civil service job, you will have to take a competitive examination made up of a general intelligence test and tests of specialized knowledge and skills.

This chapter will provide many helpful suggestions on preparing for and taking such tests.

What Can Tests Tell You?

From tests you can learn many important things about yourself—your achievements, aptitudes, and interests, for example. You can learn where you stand in English, mathematics, social studies, or science in comparison with other students throughout the nation who took the same tests. You can also learn whether you are high, average, or low in academic ability or general intelligence and in special abilities; these may include the ability to express yourself in words, skill with numbers, or mechanical or clerical ability. You can learn what your interests are—music, books, art, working outdoors, working with groups of people or alone, making things with your hands. You can get valuable ideas as to what college to attend, what field to major in, and what career to prepare for.

What Kinds of Tests Are There?

In junior high and your three years of high school you probably will take more than a hundred tests. In all probability more than 90 percent of these will be achievement tests. They may range from a ten-minute daily quiz in any one of your subjects of study to an hour-long final semester examination.

How to Prepare for a Test

The following suggestions will help make tests far less of a problem for you. Even if you're a good student, you may find ways here to do better on tests.

1. *Keep up your daily work.* Try to do every assignment as conscientiously and as promptly as possible. If you get behind in your work, make it up as soon as you can. Day-by-day preparation is the best kind of preparation for a test.

2. *Review your work regularly.* Take a few minutes every day to review what you studied or discussed in the course. Skim the appropriate textbook chapter. Then reread the notes you made either in class or in your homework. Review the textbook chapters you covered and your notes at the end of every week, as well.

3. *Review your work actively.* As you review for a test, ask yourself questions. Try to answer them. Work with a classmate. Have him make up questions to ask you. Do the same for him. Use your textbook or your notebook to correct your answers.

4. *Outline and summarize your work.* As soon as you know what chapter a test is to cover, skim those chapters and your notes on them. Change the headings within a chapter into questions—then try to answer them. Prepare an outline and summary of the content of the chapter.

5. *Get help from your teacher.* If you are having trouble understanding something that may be included in a test, ask your teacher for help. Ask while the subject is still fresh in your mind. Don't wait until you have almost forgotten what the problem or question was.

6. *Concentrate on what you don't know.* In preparing for a test, spend your time on the chapter or part of a chapter you don't understand or have difficulty remembering. In a foreign language, as suggested earlier in this book, practice the words you don't know or aren't sure of—not the words you already know.

7. *Draw up and stick to a test-study schedule.* If you're preparing for your final examinations, about two weeks beforehand work out a study schedule for intensive review. Indicate day by day the subject or subjects to be studied and the approximate hour for each. Be sure to allow the most study time for the subjects in which you are weakest. Also, try to study these subjects first during an ordinary evening of homework. Try to stick to your schedule. If after a few days you find you need more time for some subjects and less for others, change your schedule to fit your needs.

8. *Keep yourself in good physical health.* If you feel well and fresh, you are more likely to do your best than if you are ill or tired. Go into training for a test as an athlete does before a game or contest—that is, eat the right foods, get enough sleep every night, and have some wholesome recreation.

9. *Strive for good mental health.* If you study efficiently every day and get ready for a test well in advance, you'll have a calm, relaxed, confident attitude. If you not only *know* but also *know that you know* the material the test is to cover, you are likely to do better in it.

10. *Review briefly just before examination.* On the night before the examination spend no more than an hour reviewing for it. During that hour go over only the things you are most likely to forget or have trouble with. Save some time for relaxation. And go to bed early.

What about Cramming?

"Never put off till tomorrow what you can do today" is a good rule to follow in many things you do, but especially in preparing for a test. If you are like all too many students, you postpone studying for a test until the night before the test. That evening you study from seven o'clock until one or two in the morning or even later. During these last-minute hours you try to *cram* for the exam.

Cramming for a test is one of the poorest ways to prepare for it. In the first place, cramming your studying into a single, large block of time is inefficient. In the second place, cramming can wear you out. You may become too fatigued to get much help from studying. Because of lack of sleep, you may be too tired in class to do your best on the test. Short, frequent reviews are a far more effective way to prepare for a test.

How to Take a Test

In general, you will take two main kinds of tests—the essay test and the objective test. In an essay test you write, in your own words, a fairly long, well-organized, discussion-type answer to each question. Objective tests call for short, specific answers. You may, for example, be asked to fill in a blank with the correct answer, or write down the letter or number for the correct one of several answers given. In some instances you make only a check mark to answer an item.

Other important differences between these two kinds of tests are as follows: *First,* because objective questions don't require lengthy answers, objective tests usually have many more questions than essay tests, perhaps a hundred or more, as compared with ten or twenty essay questions. *Second,* in an essay test the teacher may score your answers as fully right, partly right, or fully wrong. In an objective test he scores your answers as either right or wrong.

Your teacher may give you a final examination that is made up of both kinds of items—many objective items that test your knowledge of the content of the field, and a few essay items that test your ability to organize that knowledge in written form.

How to Take an Essay Test

In an essay test the teacher presents one or more items that are questions or statements to which you are to respond—for example, *Give five reasons why the North was able to defeat the South in the Civil War.*

In answering an essay test item, you express your knowledge or ideas in essay or outline form. Your teacher will mark your answer on the basis of the quality of what you write, not the quantity. You may write as much or as little as you wish and have the time for. In general, though, you should keep your answers brief and to the point.

In addition, keep in mind the following points:

1. *Read all the items in an essay test* before you begin to answer the first one. Skimming the test as a whole gives you a clearer idea of the content covered. You also start thinking about each of the items, how they are related to each other, and possible overlapping. In this way you will learn whether you are expected to answer all the questions or whether there is some choice, and whether some questions count for more than others.

2. *Answer test items in the order of their appearance.* In a well-organized test the teacher may arrange essay questions from the easiest to the hardest. If he has done so, you should answer item 1, then item 2, then item 3.

3. If you come across *a particularly difficult test item, skip it temporarily*—and later go back to it. If you spend too much time on a difficult question, you won't have enough for the others. As you answer the other questions, however, reserve time for the one that gave you trouble. When you return to it, you may find it is easier than you thought. Also, your answers to the other questions may help you with this one.

4. *Budget your time.* As you first read the whole examination, estimate how much time you should spend on each item. If the test has five items and you have fifty minutes to answer them, for instance, you can spend an average of ten minutes on each item. However, the more difficult an item is—or the more points it counts for—the more time you should allow for it. While you are taking the test, glance at the clock from time to time to see how many minutes you have left. Try to answer *all* the test items as well as you can during the available time.

5. *Read each test item carefully.* If the item is in the form of an instruction, it will start with a verb such as *describe, explain, list,* or *compare.* Do exactly what this verb tells you to do.

To illustrate how the instructions in test items may vary, here are some examples from an American history test:

1. Describe the chief differences in the ways people lived in the North and in the South before the Civil War.

2. Explain how the Underground Railroad worked.

3. List five events that touched off the Civil War.

4. Compare economic conditions in the North and in the South after the Civil War.

In the items just given, note carefully not only the verbs but also the key phrases that follow the verbs: *the chief differences; five events; economic conditions.* If an item asks for chief differences, give these differences. Do *not* give causes or events. And do not give *minor* differences. If an item asks for *five* events, give five causes. Present these in the order of their importance.

To sum up this point—before you answer a

test item, always read it carefully at least twice. Be sure you understand the questions and directions. Think before you write.

6. *Make an outline of your answer.* Jot down your ideas and then organize them. List them in brief rough form on scratch paper. Leave plenty of space between ideas so that you can make changes. Organize these ideas in the form of an outline—the main ideas and the supporting ideas. If necessary, change the order of the ideas by writing a new number near each item. Then use this working outline to write your answer to the item on your test paper. If you follow the suggestion just given, you won't waste time copying and recopying your ideas before writing your final answer.

7. *Write your answer to each test item as briefly as you can* without omitting necessary facts. Put in only the essentials. Don't include ideas that relate only vaguely to the question. Don't pad your answer; stick to the point.

8. *Write your answers legibly.* That is, write so that your teacher can easily read your answer without eyestrain and without guessing. Obviously, if your teacher can't read your handwritten answer, he can't give you credit for it.

9. *Use correct and appropriate language.* Make certain that the subject and predicate in each sentence agree in number and that the tenses of your verbs are consistent. Check on your spelling, capitalization, and punctuation. In general, don't use slang. If you use correct English, your teacher is more likely to give you full credit for your answers. If you make mistakes in English, he may deduct points from your total test score.

10. After you answer all the test items, *reread and edit your test paper.* Be sure you have answered all the test items and all their parts, if any have more than one part. Read your paper to correct or improve its content, to correct errors in grammar and language usage, and to catch errors in spelling, capitalization, and punctuation.

How to Take Objective Tests

The different types of objective tests, in the order of their frequency of use, are (1) multiple-choice, (2) matching (a variation of multiple-choice), (3) classification, (4) completion, (5) true-false, and (6) rearrangement.

Here are examples of each type:

1. *Multiple-choice* (In a multiple-choice item you are given the first part of a statement and several choices with which to complete the statement. One of these choices is correct; the others are incorrect.)

To *assemble* materials means to
_____a. make them look alike
_____b. report on them
_____c. gather them in one place
_____d. read about them
_____e. destroy them

2. *Matching* (In a matching test you are presented with two lists of items. Items in one list are to be matched with items in the other list: authors with their books, events with their dates, rules of grammar with their applications, scientific terms with their definitions, names of places with their locations on a map.)

Match the authors with their works. At the left of each author's name write the letter that indicates the book or play he wrote.

_____William Shakespeare a. *A Christmas*
_____Charles Dickens   *Carol*
_____Mark Twain   b. *Romeo and Juliet*
                        c. *Adventures of Tom Sawyer*
                        d. *Little Women*
                        e. *Robinson Crusoe*

3. *Classification* (In a classification test item you are given a number of objects or ideas that belong in the same group or class and one that does not. You are to identify the one that does not.)

Mark a check at the left of the correct choice. Which animal does not belong with the others?

_____a. Ape   _____d. Shark
_____b. Elephant   _____e. Whale
_____c. Kangaroo

4. *Completion* (In a completion test item you are given part of a sentence that you are to complete. This type of item is best for testing your ability to remember or recognize a specific

94

fact such as a date, name, event, or scientific or mathematical formula. It does not do a very good job of testing your ability to interpret a complex idea.)

Write the correct answer on the blank line.

The first ten amendments to the Constitution of the United States are known as _____ _____.

5. *True-false* (In a true-false test item you are given a statement. You are to decide whether it is true or false. Some items may contain qualifying words such as *all, none, always, never.* An item that has such a cue word is frequently false. If a statement has the word *must,* it is usually false. If it has the word *might* or *may,* it is usually true.)

If the statement is true, write a + at the left of it. If the statement is false, write a 0 at the left of it.

_____The president of the United States is commander in chief of the armed forces.

6. *Rearrangement* (In a rearrangement test you are presented with a group of items that you are to number in the correct order—for instance, cities in the order of their population size, events in the order of their importance. This type of test is a good measure of your ability to recall or to judge the relation of one thing to another.)

Number the following cities in order, beginning with the city with the largest population and ending with the city with the smallest population.

_____Chicago   _____New York
_____Los Angeles   _____Philadelphia

(Answers are at the end of the chapter.)

Of the six types of objective tests just illustrated, the multiple-choice type is most widely used. It is among the best because it can be used to measure not only knowledge of facts but also understanding of complex ideas.

General Suggestions for Taking Any Type of Test

In taking an essay or an objective test, you may find the following summary helpful:

1. Be sure you have pencil, pen, eraser, pa-per, and any other materials you will need for the test.

2. Read the test directions carefully. Follow them exactly.

3. On an essay test read all items and budget your time for them. Skip difficult items and go back to them later.

4. Answer each item as instructed. Don't write unrelated material.

5. Reread your test paper to correct any errors.

6. Your first impression is usually correct. Therefore, think twice before you completely change your answer to a test item.

How to Follow Up a Test

Your teacher will give you a percentage or letter grade on your test paper. He will also indicate which questions you answered incorrectly or incompletely. Your next step is to follow up and find out why you made the mistakes you did. Did you misunderstand a question or read it incorrectly? Did you simply not know the answer? Look up the correct answers to all the questions you missed. Study them carefully. If there is something you still don't understand, discuss it with your teacher.

This kind of follow-up will help you learn more about the subject. Also, you will probably do better on the next test.

Before you close this book, a final check:

To determine the progress you have made in your study skills, habits, and attitudes as a result of working in this book, mark your answers to the checklist in chapter 1 again. Next, compare your answers then with your answers now. On how many items have your study habits improved? Reread the items you answered *negatively.* For each of the study abilities indicated by these items, you should continue your efforts to improve—to become a better student.

● **Answers** to exercises in this chapter:
1—c; 2—William Shakespeare, b; Charles Dickens, a; Mark Twain, c; 3—d; 4—the Bill of Rights; 5—+; 6—New York (1), Chicago (2), Los Angeles (3), Philadelphia (4).